Eizo Nishio

Paintings & Sculptures 2019-2020

Art & Books

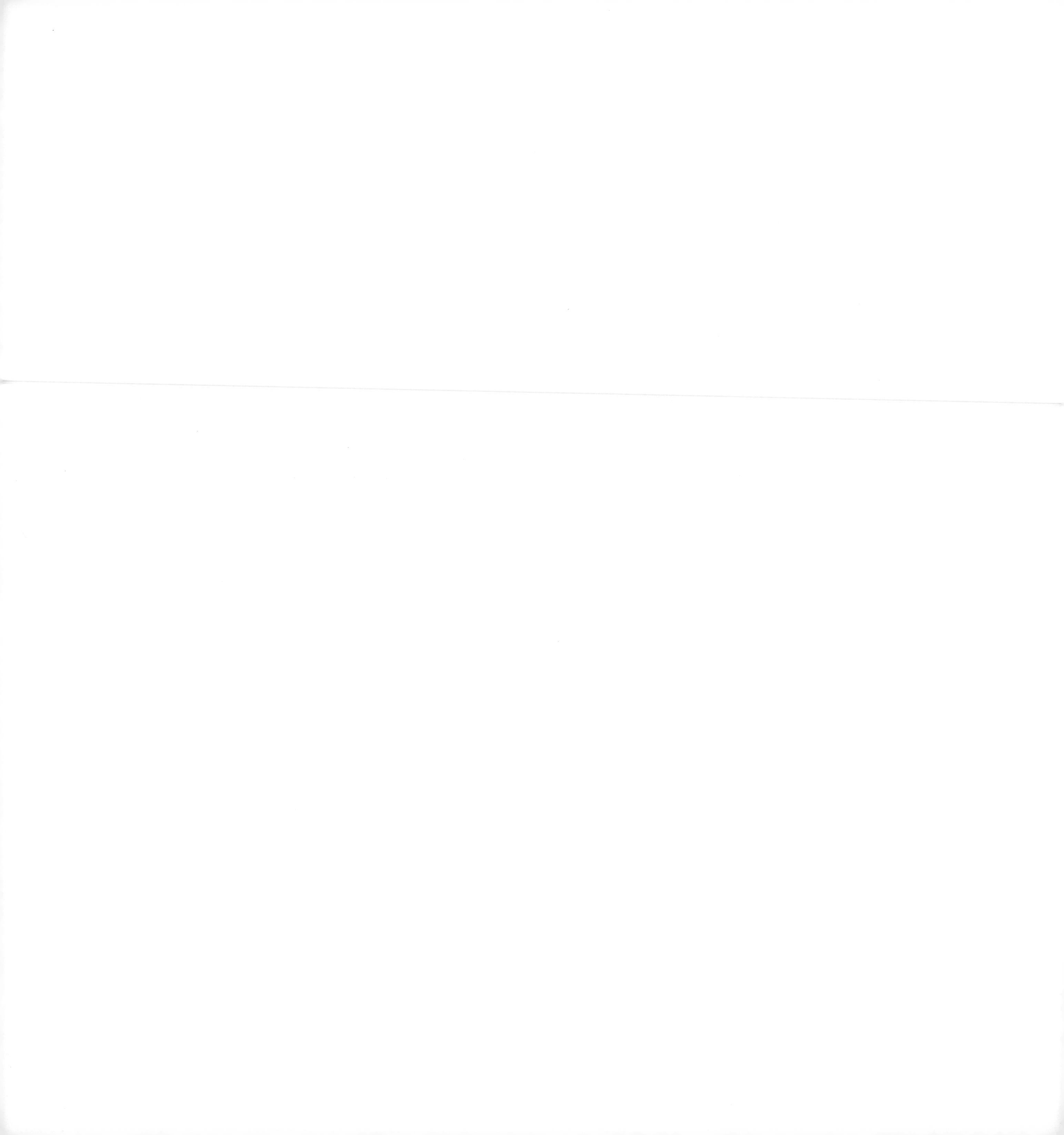

Contents

Painting

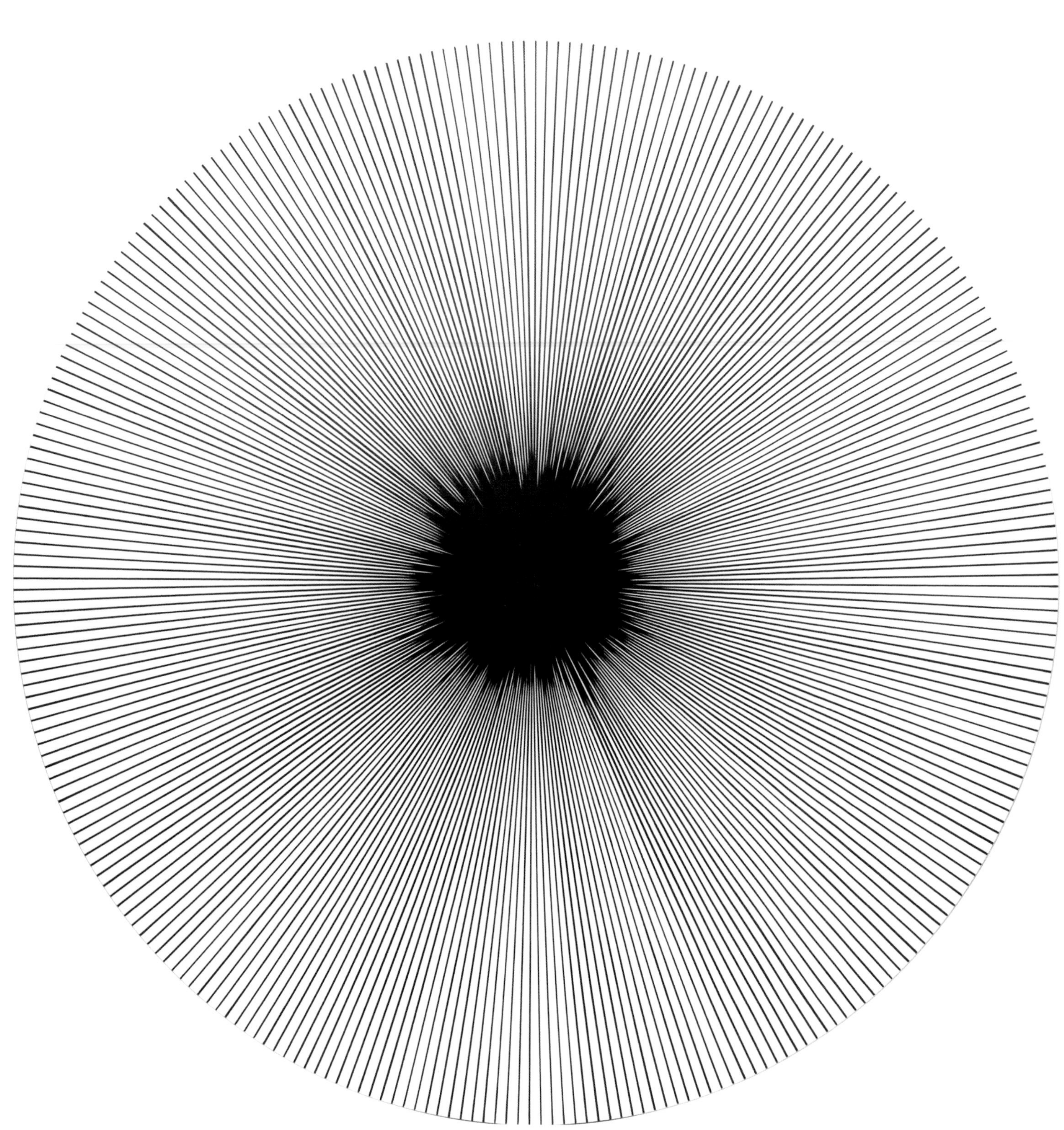

Black hole I
2019
acrylic on aluminum plate
diameter 90 cm / 35.4 in.

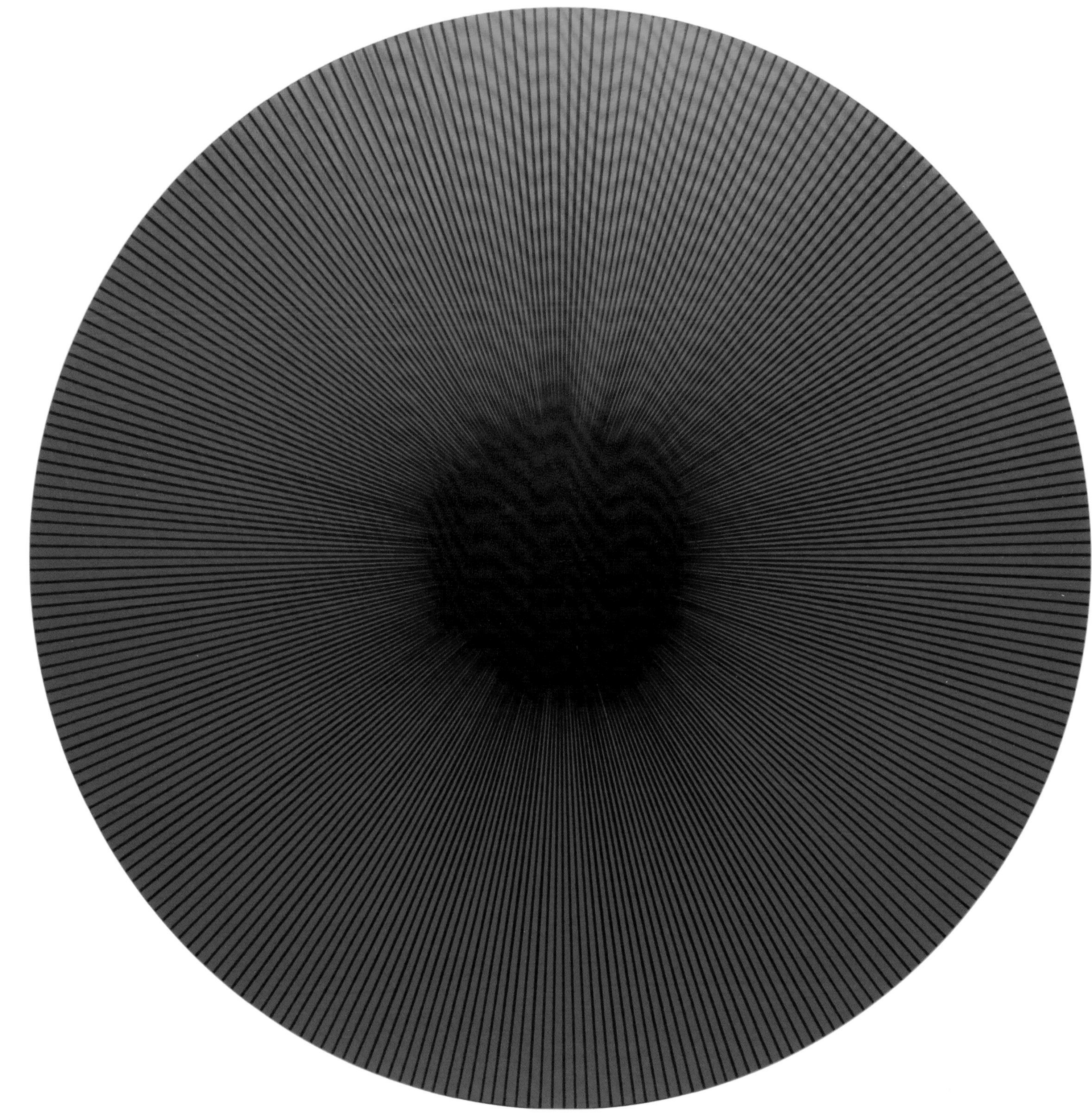

Black hole XII
2019
acrylic on aluminum plate
diameter 90 cm / 35.4 in.

The Big Bang I
2019
acrylic on aluminum plate
diameter 90 cm / 35.4 in.

The Big Bang VII
2019
acrylic on aluminum plate
diameter 90 cm / 35.4 in.

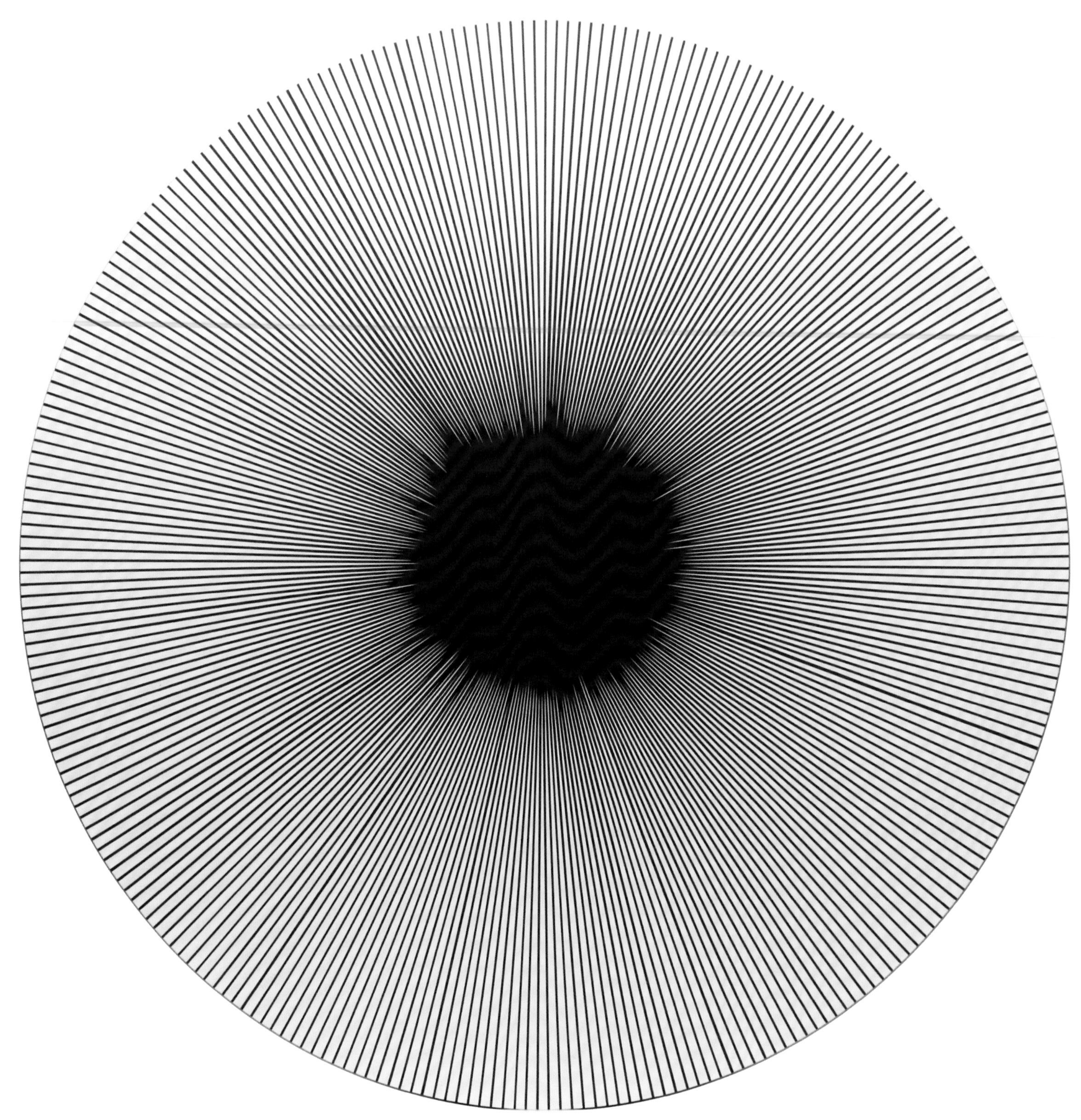

Black hole VI
2019
acrylic on aluminum plate
diameter 90 cm / 35.4 in.

Black hole IX
2020
acrylic on aluminum plate
diameter 90 cm / 35.4 in.

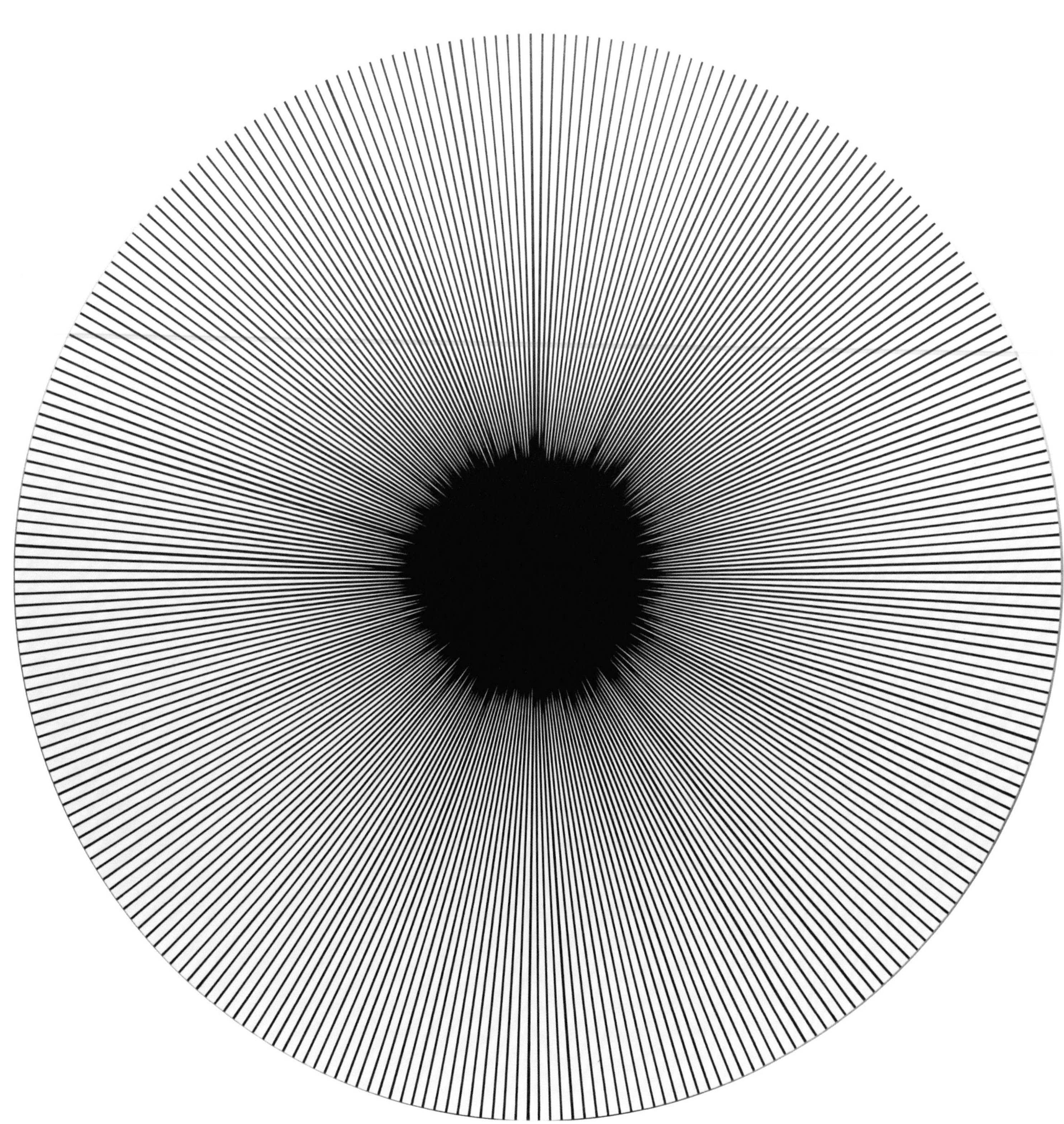

Black hole XI
2019
acrylic on aluminum plate
diameter 90 cm / 35.4 in.

Black hole IV
2019
acrylic on aluminum plate
diameter 90 cm / 35.4 in.

The Big Bang V
2019
acrylic on aluminum plate
diameter 90 cm / 35.4 in.

Black hole III
2019
acrylic on aluminum plate
diameter 90 cm / 35.4 in.

The Big Bang III
2019
acrylic on aluminum plate
diameter 90 cm / 35.4 in.

The Big Bang II
2019
acrylic on aluminum plate
diameter 90 cm / 35.4 in.

The Big Bang IV
2019
acrylic on aluminum plate
diameter 90 cm / 35.4 in.

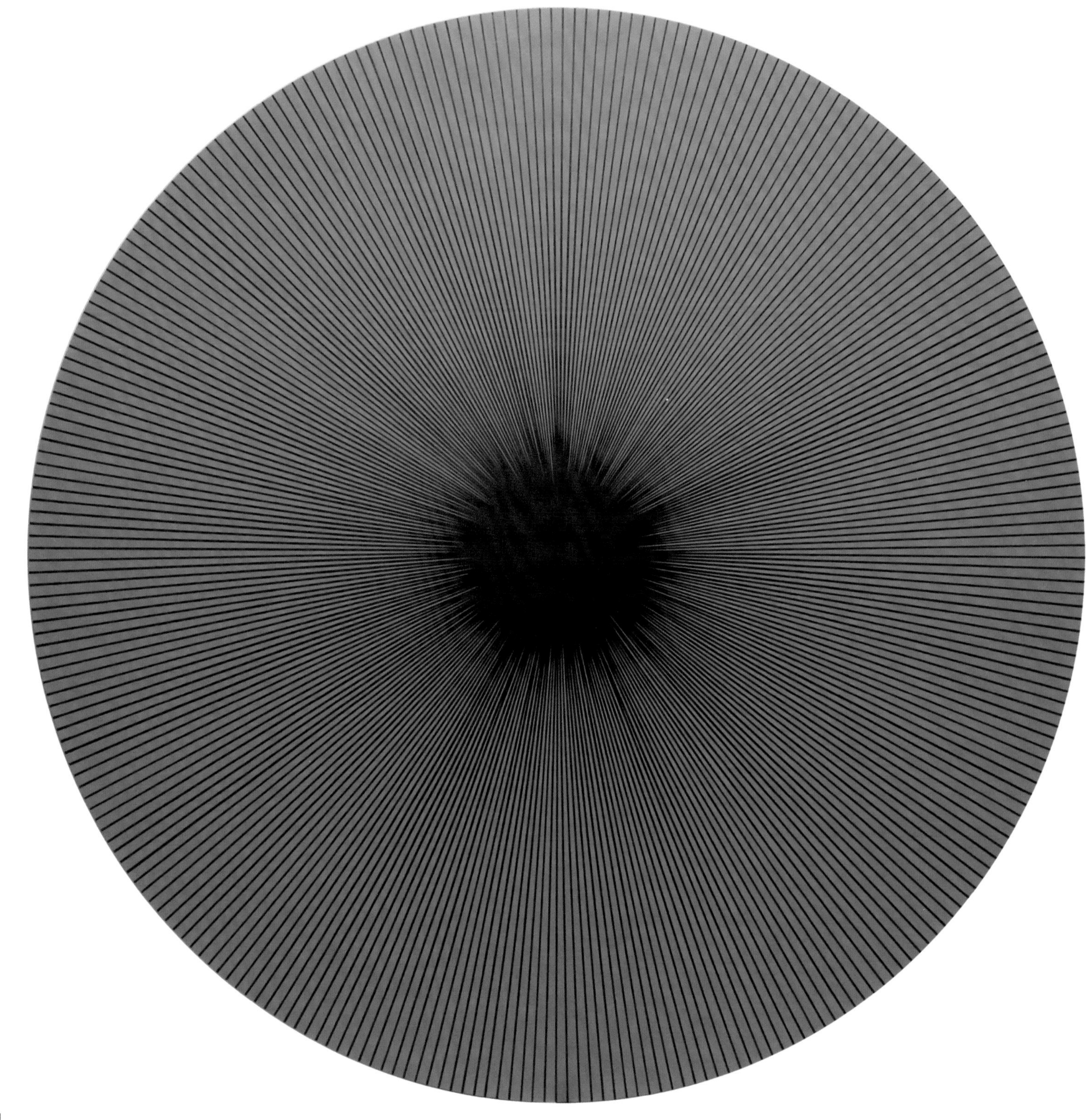

Black hole II
2019
acrylic on aluminum plate
diameter 90 cm / 35.4 in.

The Big Bang VI
2019
acrylic on aluminum plate
diameter 90 cm / 35.4 in.

The Big Bang IX
2019
acrylic on aluminum plate
diameter 90 cm / 35.4 in.

Black hole V
2019
acrylic on aluminum plate
diameter 90 cm / 35.4 in.

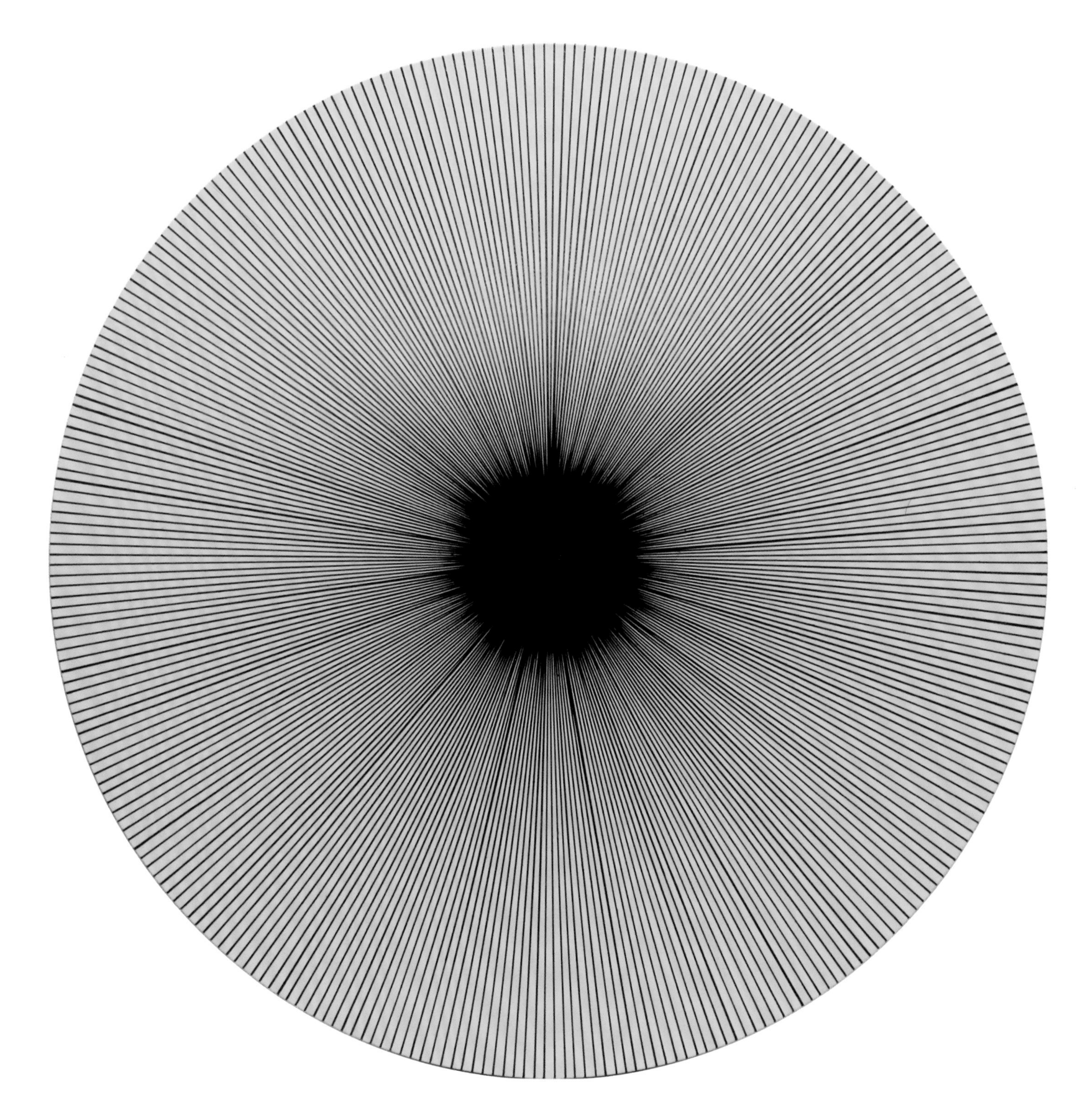

Small Black hole Yellow
2019
acrylic on aluminum plate
diameter 52 cm / 20.5 in.

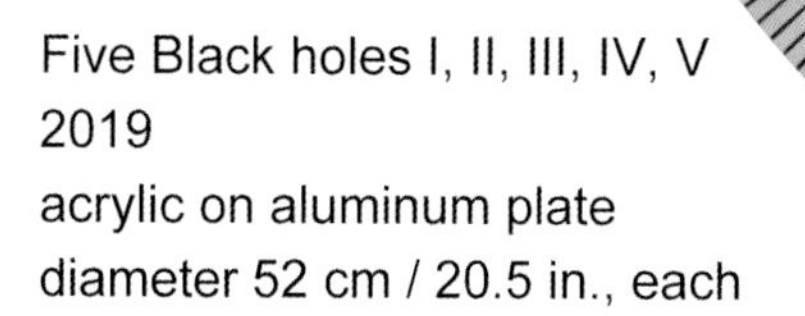

Five Black holes I, II, III, IV, V
2019
acrylic on aluminum plate
diameter 52 cm / 20.5 in., each

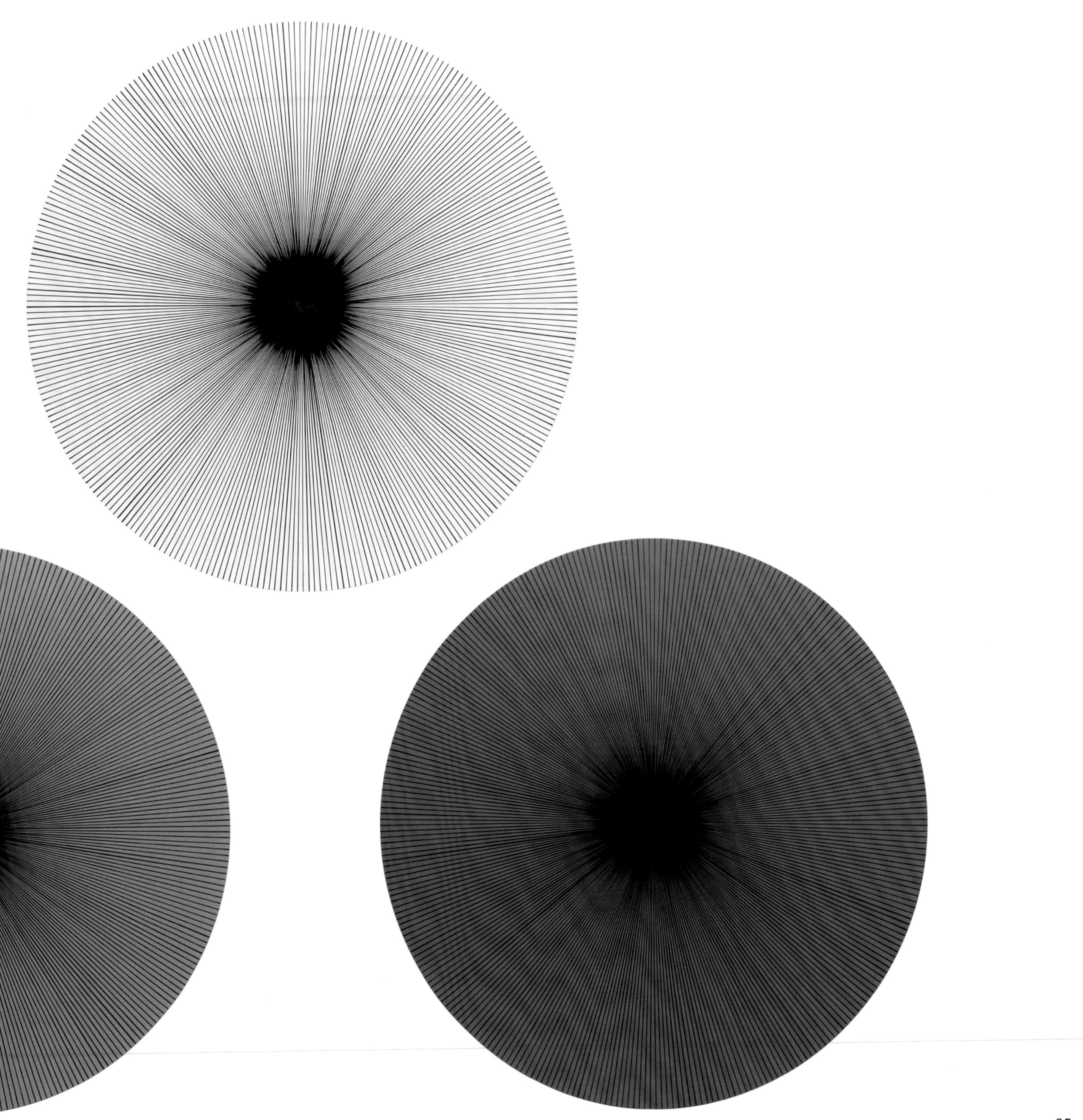

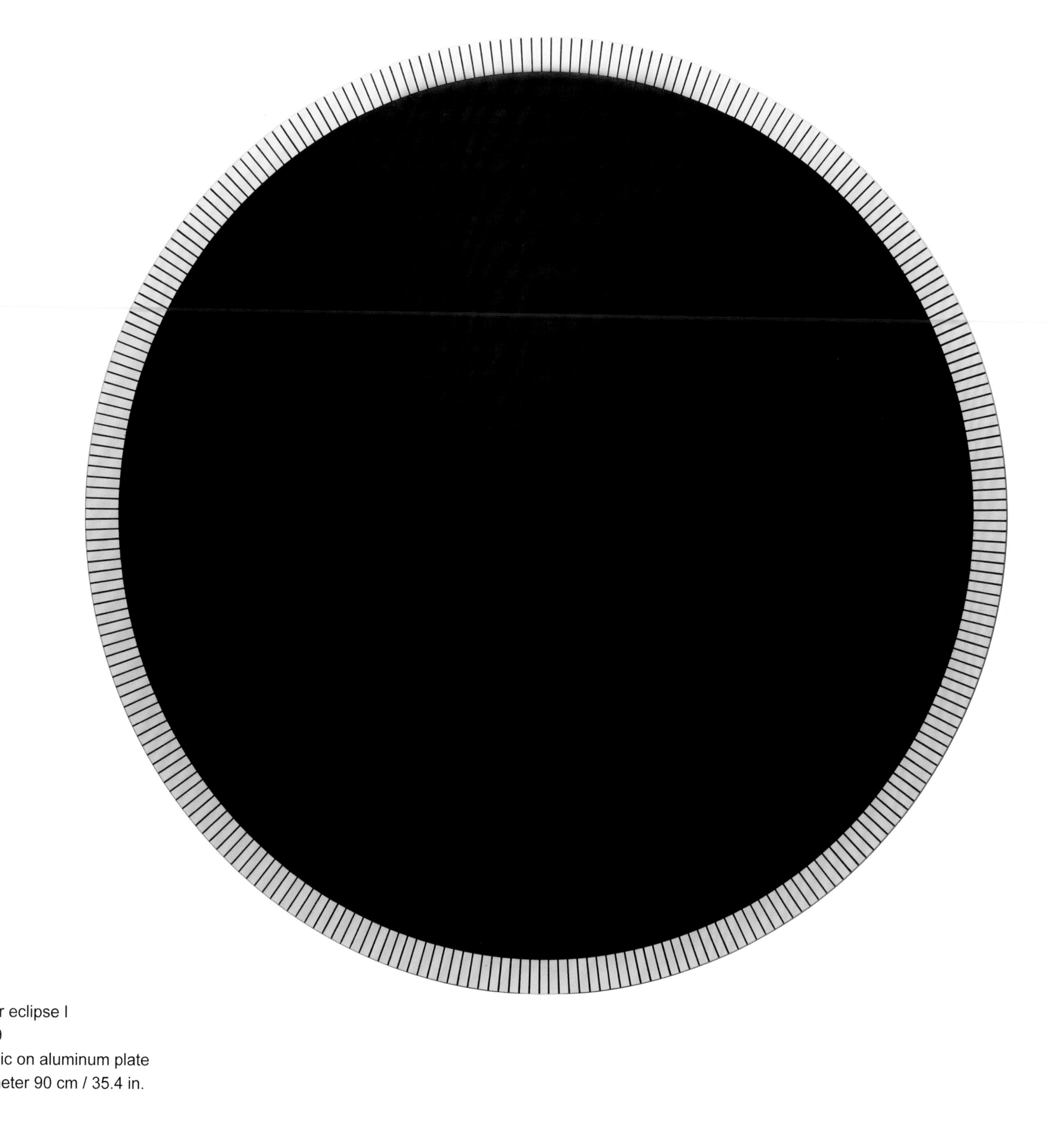

Solar eclipse I
2019
acrylic on aluminum plate
diameter 90 cm / 35.4 in.

Solar eclipse III
2019
acrylic on aluminum plate
diameter 90 cm / 35.4 in.

Solar eclipse II
2019
acrylic on aluminum plate
diameter 90 cm / 35.4 in.

Abstract Expressionism 21C VI, 2019
acrylic on aluminum plate, 83 x 71 cm / 32.7 x 28 in.

Abstract Expressionism 21C IX, 2019
acrylic on aluminum plate, 83 x 71 cm / 32.7 x 28 in.

Abstract Expressionism 21C VII, 2019
acrylic on aluminum plate, 83 x 71 cm / 32.7 x 28 in.

Abstract Expressionism 21C VIII, 2019
acrylic on aluminum plate, 83 x 71 cm / 32.7 x 28 in.

Abstract Expressionism 21C X, 2019
acrylic on aluminum plate, 83 x 71 cm / 32.7 x 28 in.

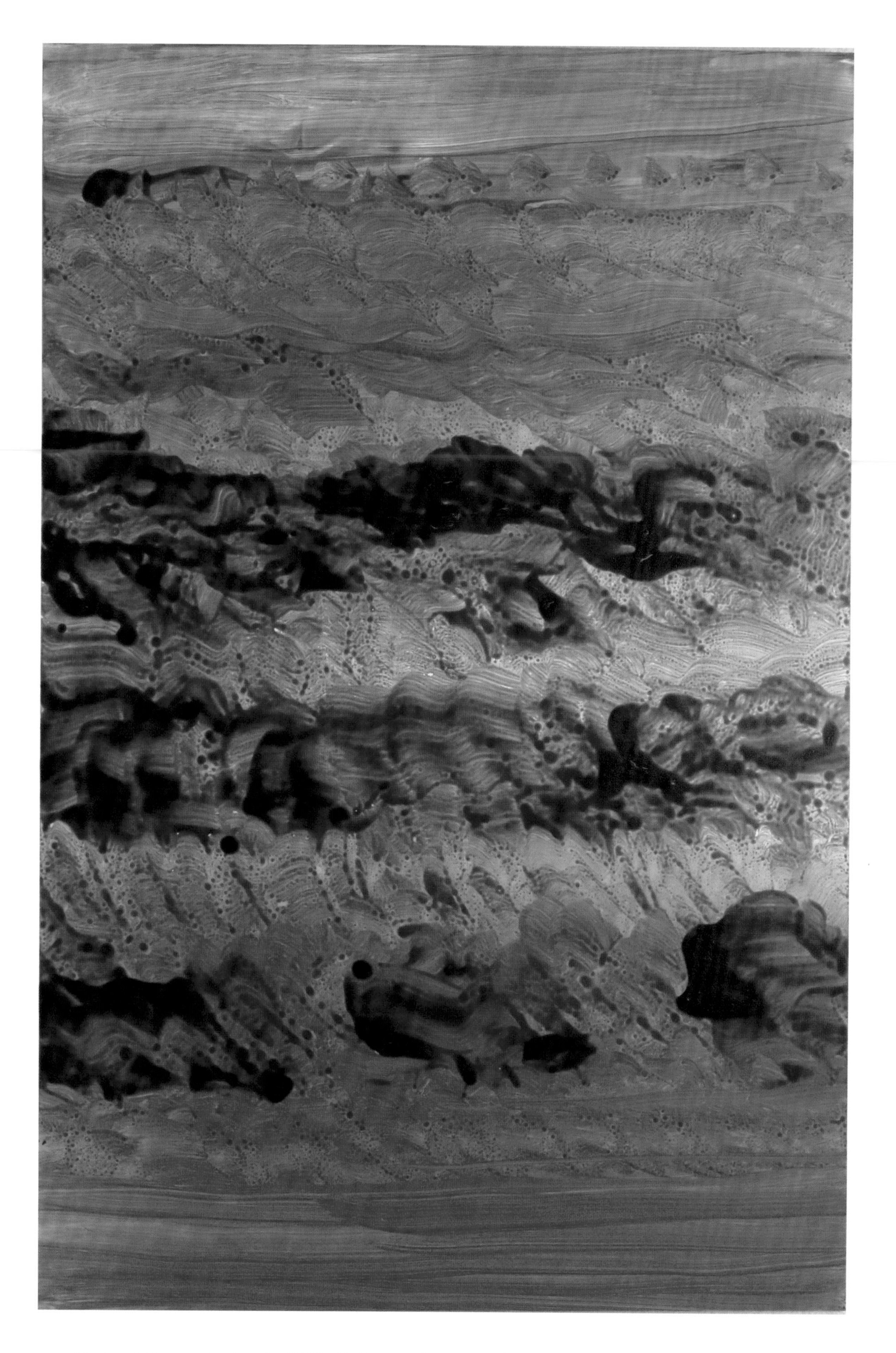

Abstract Expressionism 21C XII, 2019, acrylic on aluminum plate, 60 x 40 cm / 23.6 x 15.7 in.

Abstract Expressionism 21C XI, 2019, acrylic on aluminum plate, 60 x 40 cm / 23.6 x 15.7 in.

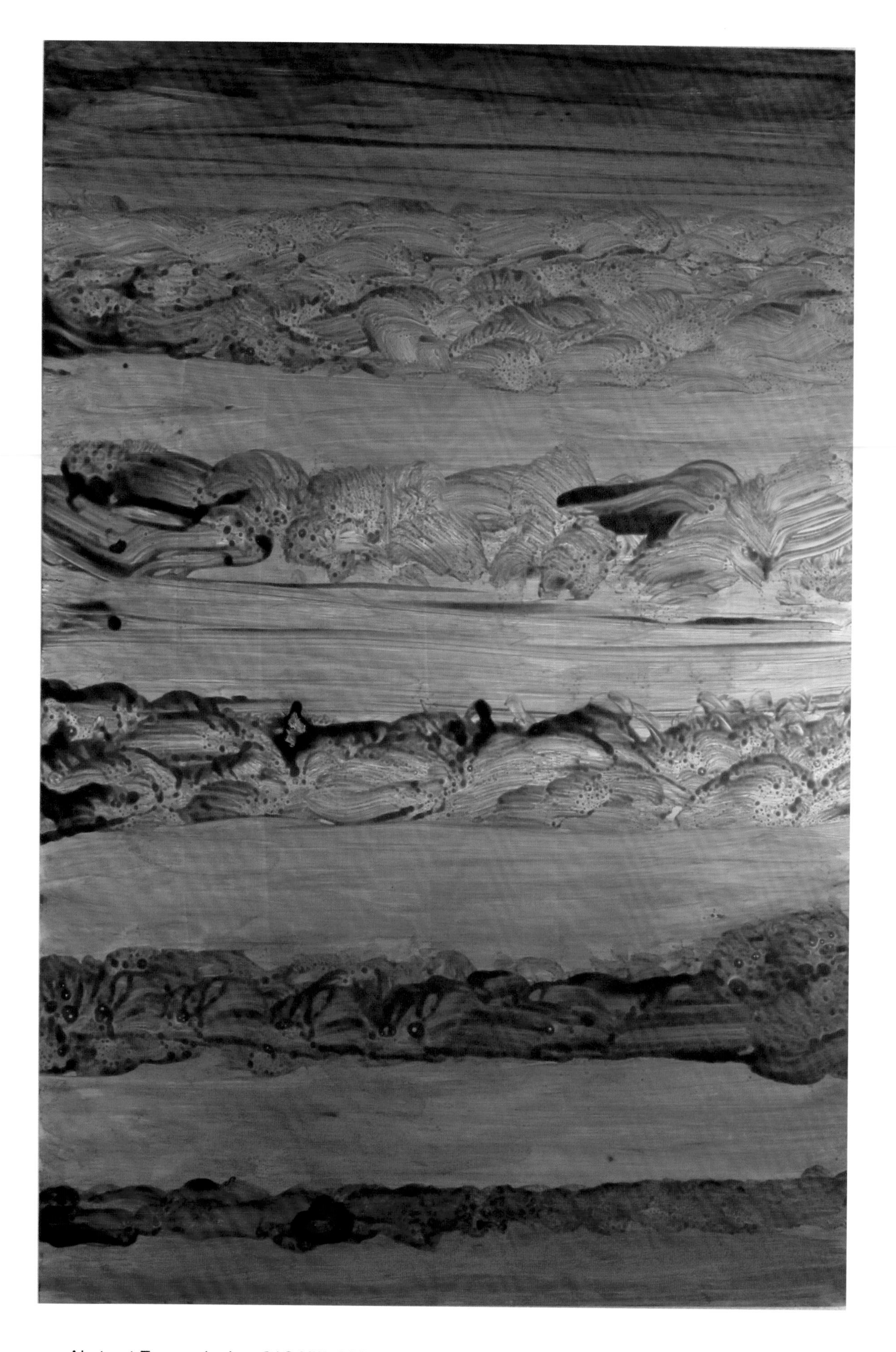

Abstract Expressionism 21C XIII, 2019, acrylic on aluminum plate, 60 x 40 cm / 23.6 x 15.7 in.

Abstract Expressionism 21C XIV, 2019, acrylic on aluminum plate, 60 x 40 cm / 23.6 x 15.7 in.

Abstract Expressionism 21C I, 2019
acrylic on aluminum plate, 83 x 79 cm / 32.7 x 31.1 in.

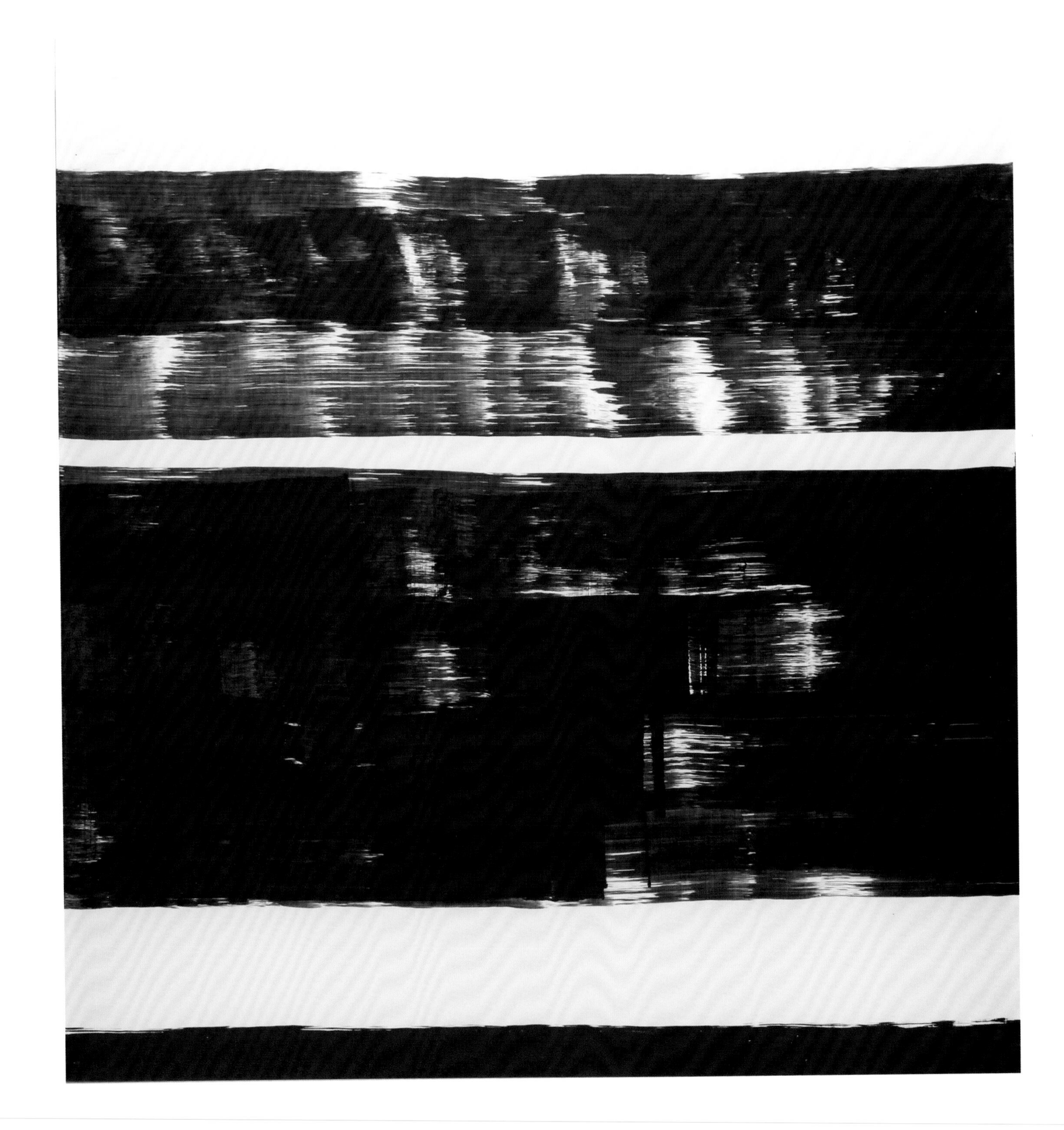

Abstract Expressionism 21C II, 2019
acrylic on aluminum plate, 83 x 79 cm / 32.7 x 31.1 in.

Abstract Expressionism 21C IV, 2019
acrylic on aluminum plate, 83 x 79 cm / 32.7 x 31.1 in.

Abstract Expressionism 21C V, 2019
acrylic on aluminum plate, 83 x 79 cm / 32.7 x 31.1 in.

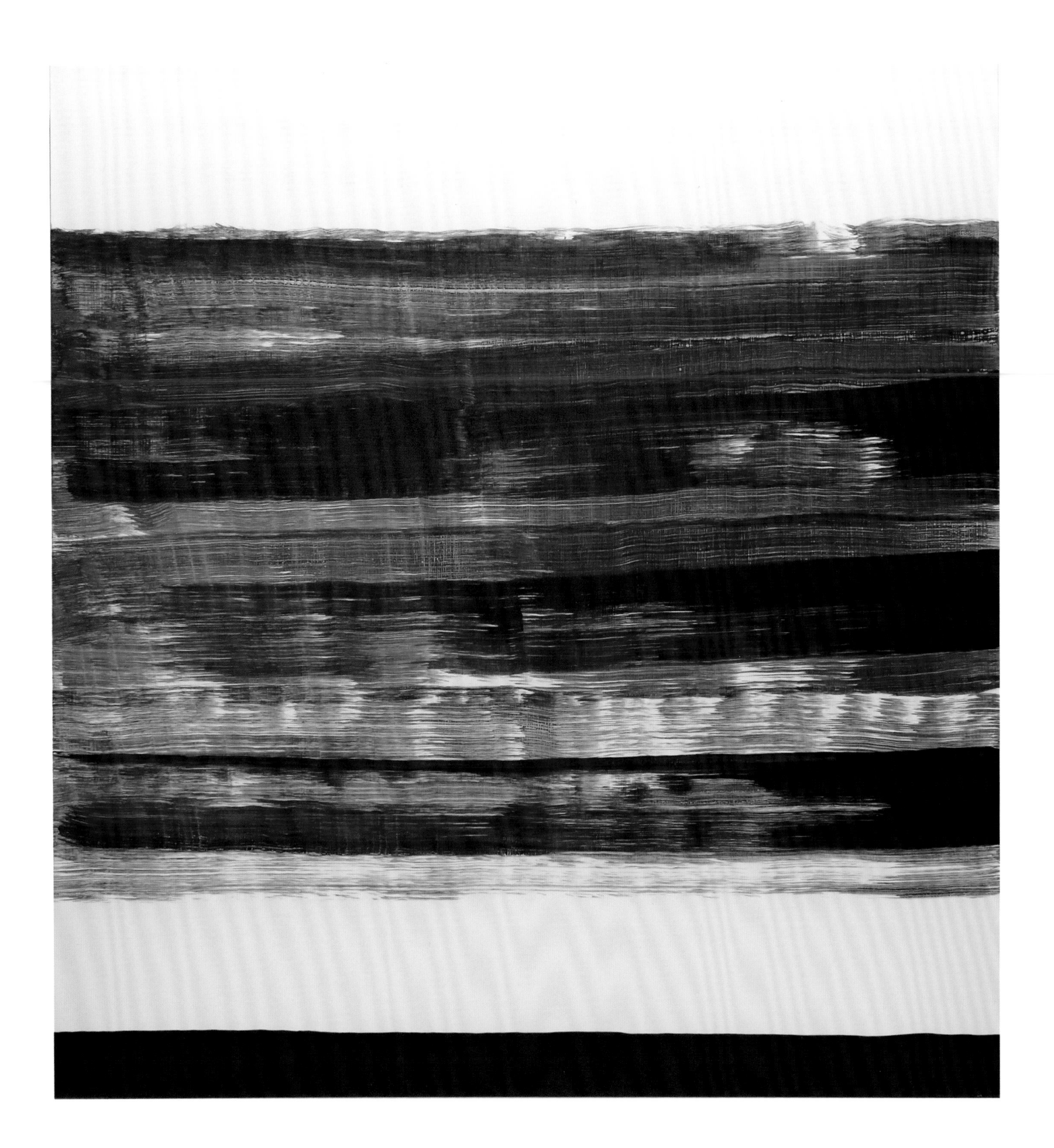

Abstract Expressionism 21C III, 2019
acrylic on aluminum plate, 83 x 79 cm / 32.7 x 31.1 in.

Composition I, 2019
acrylic on aluminum plate, 36 x 36 cm / 14.2 x 14.2 in.

Composition II, III, IV
2019
acrylic on aluminum plate
II: 9 x 54 cm / 3.5 x 21.3 in.
III: 12 x 72 cm / 4.7 x 28.3 in.
IV: 9 x 36 cm / 3.5 x 14.2 in.

Frame Painting I
2019
acrylic on aluminum plate
26.2 x 38 cm / 10.3 x 15 in.

Frame Painting II
2019
acrylic on aluminum plate
26.2 x 38 cm / 10.3 x 15 in.

Frame Painting III
2019
acrylic on aluminum plate
26.2 x 38 cm / 10.3 x 15 in.

Frame Painting IV
2019
acrylic on aluminum plate
26.2 x 38 cm / 10.3 x 15 in.

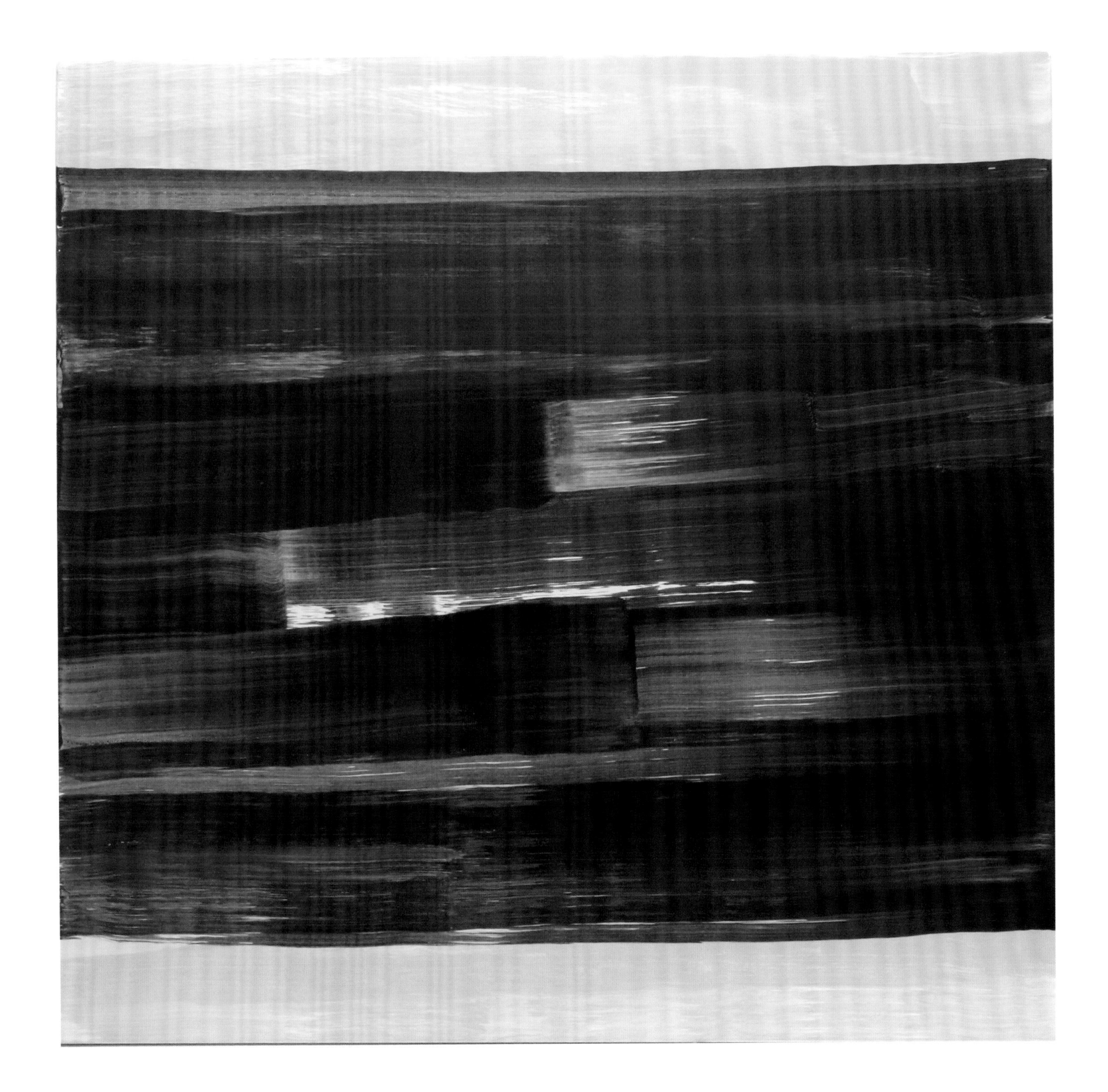

Works on Paper Viridian Hue, 2019
acrylic on cardboard, 59.4 x 62.5 cm / 23.4 x 24.6 in.

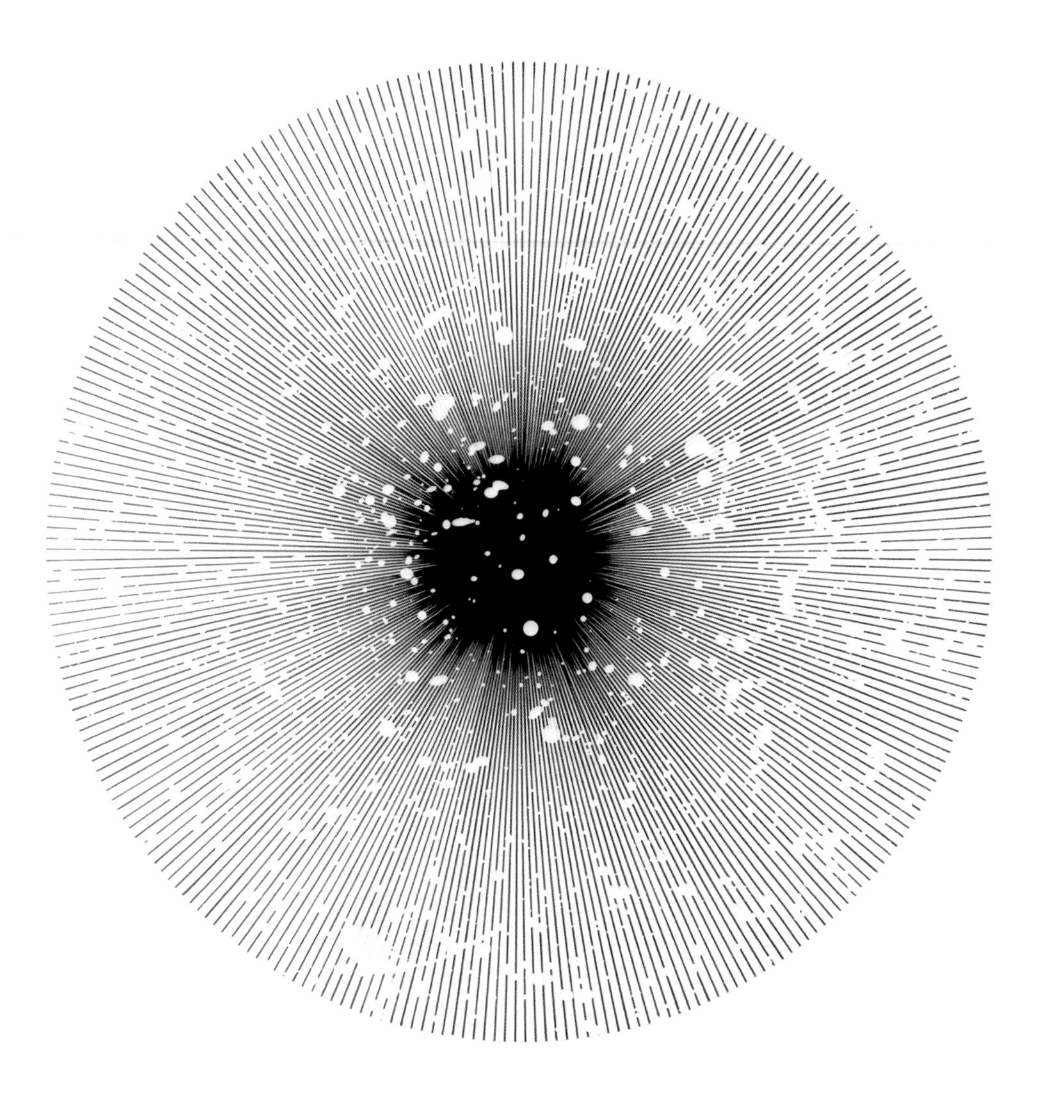

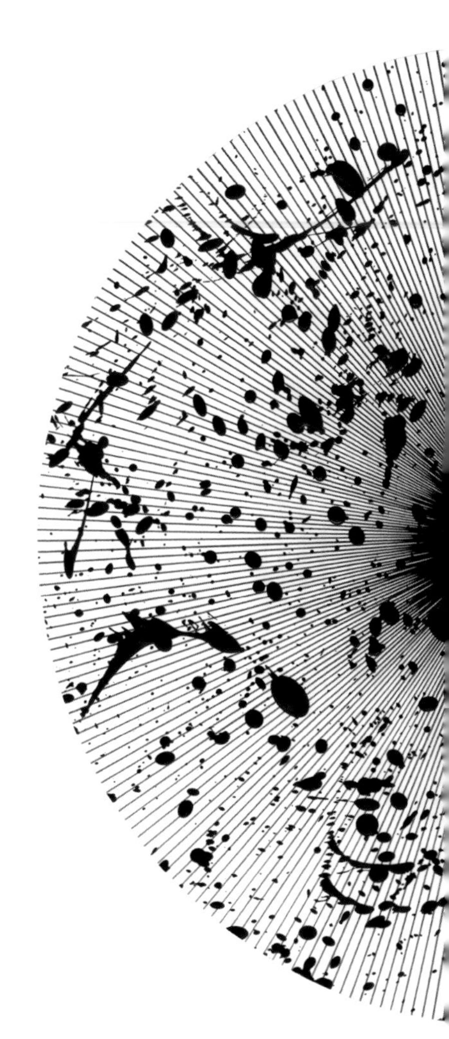

Black hole Drawing I, II, III
2019
acrylic on paper, inkjet print
diameter 25.7 cm / 10.1 in., each

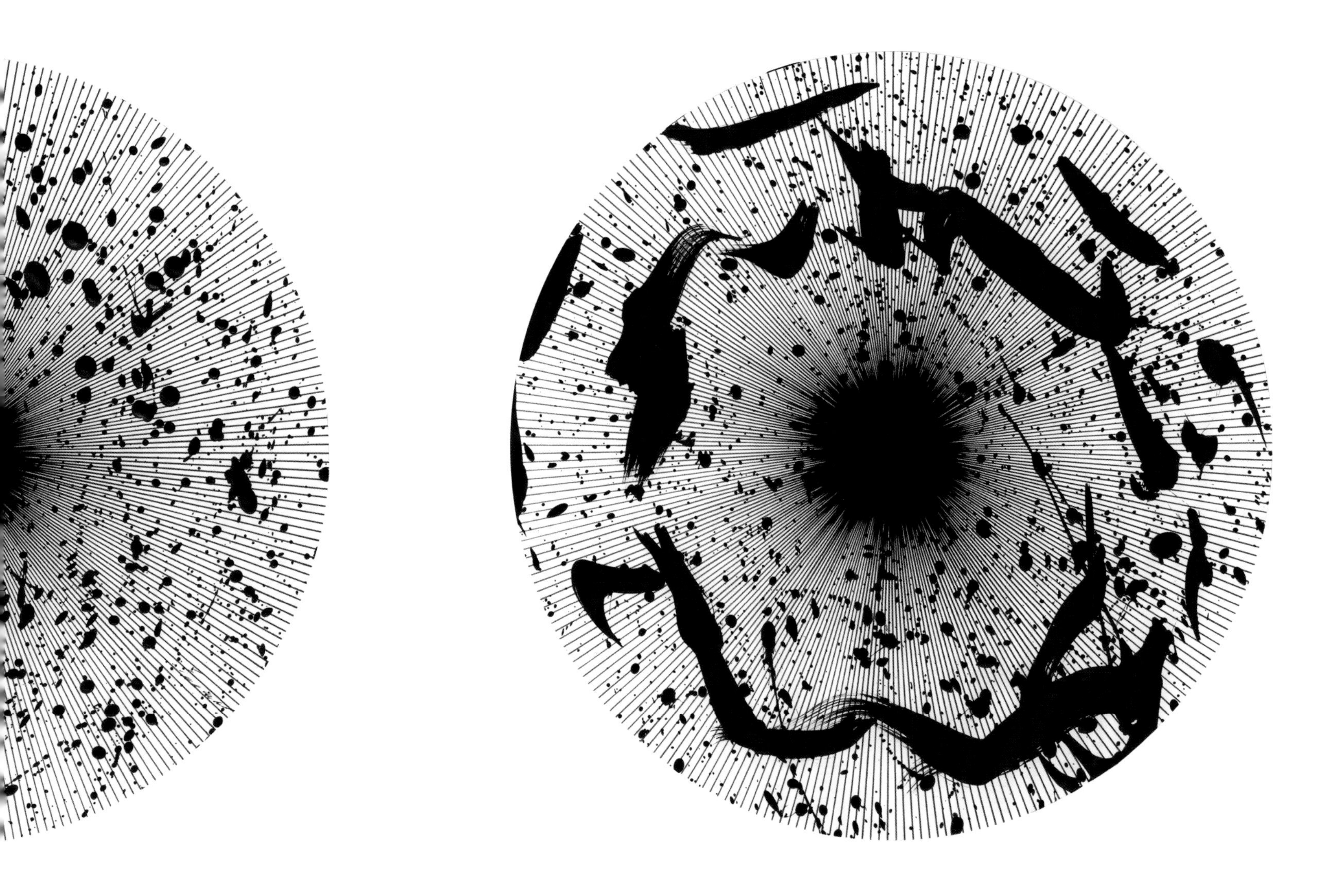

Sculpture

Photographs by Eizo Nishio

Sculpture XXVII (Wall III)
2019

Sculpture XXVIII (Wall IV)
2019

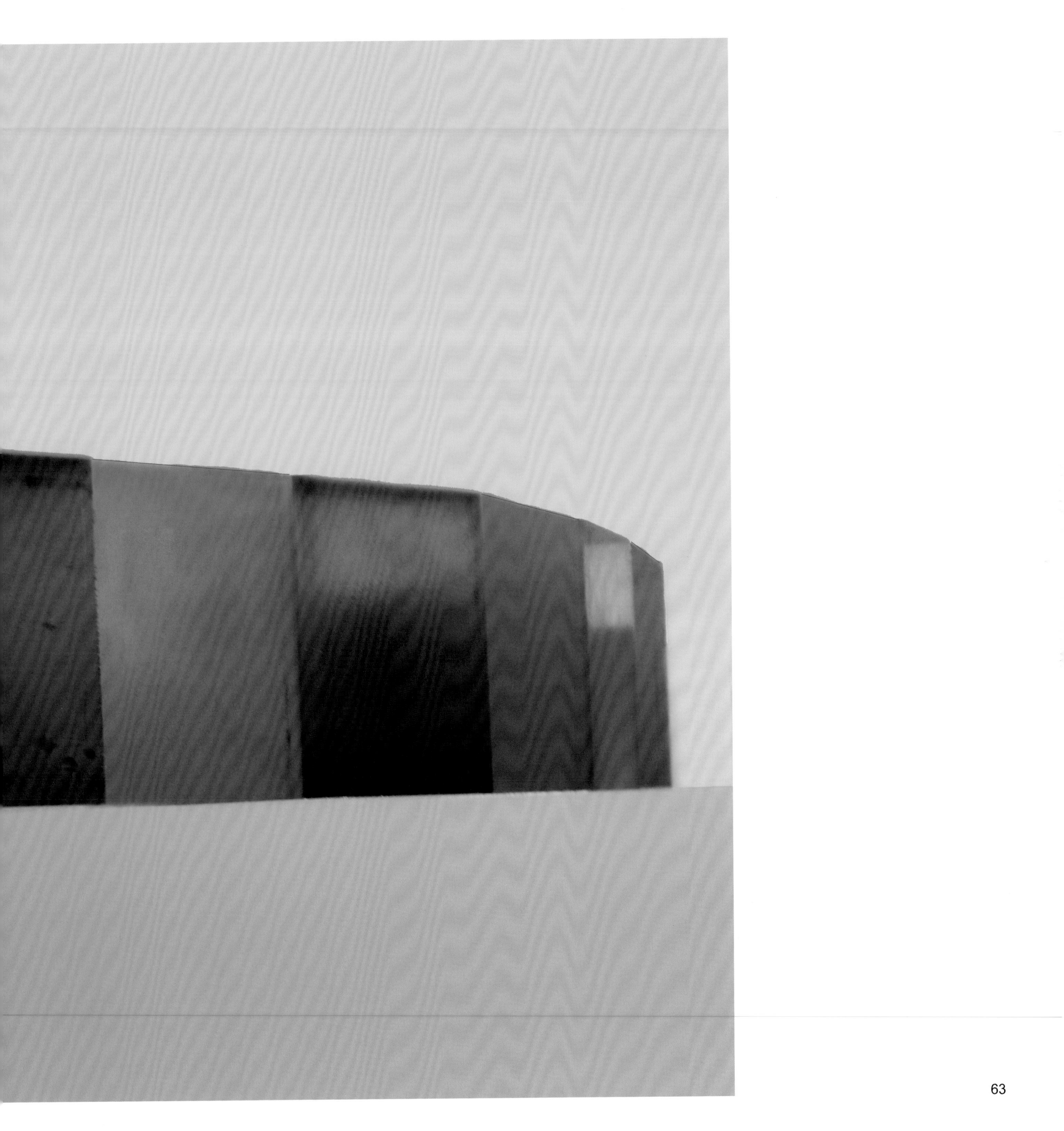

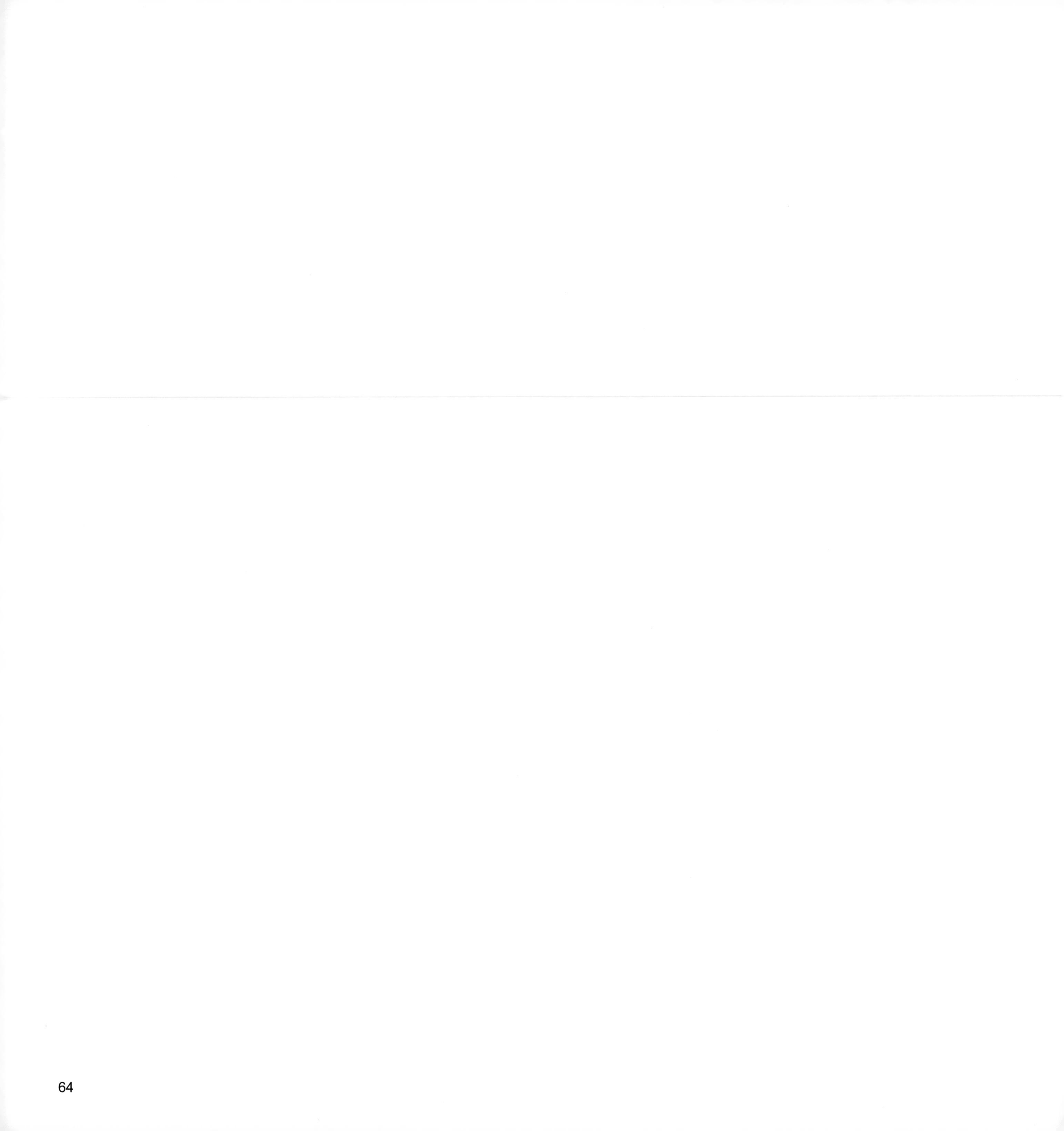

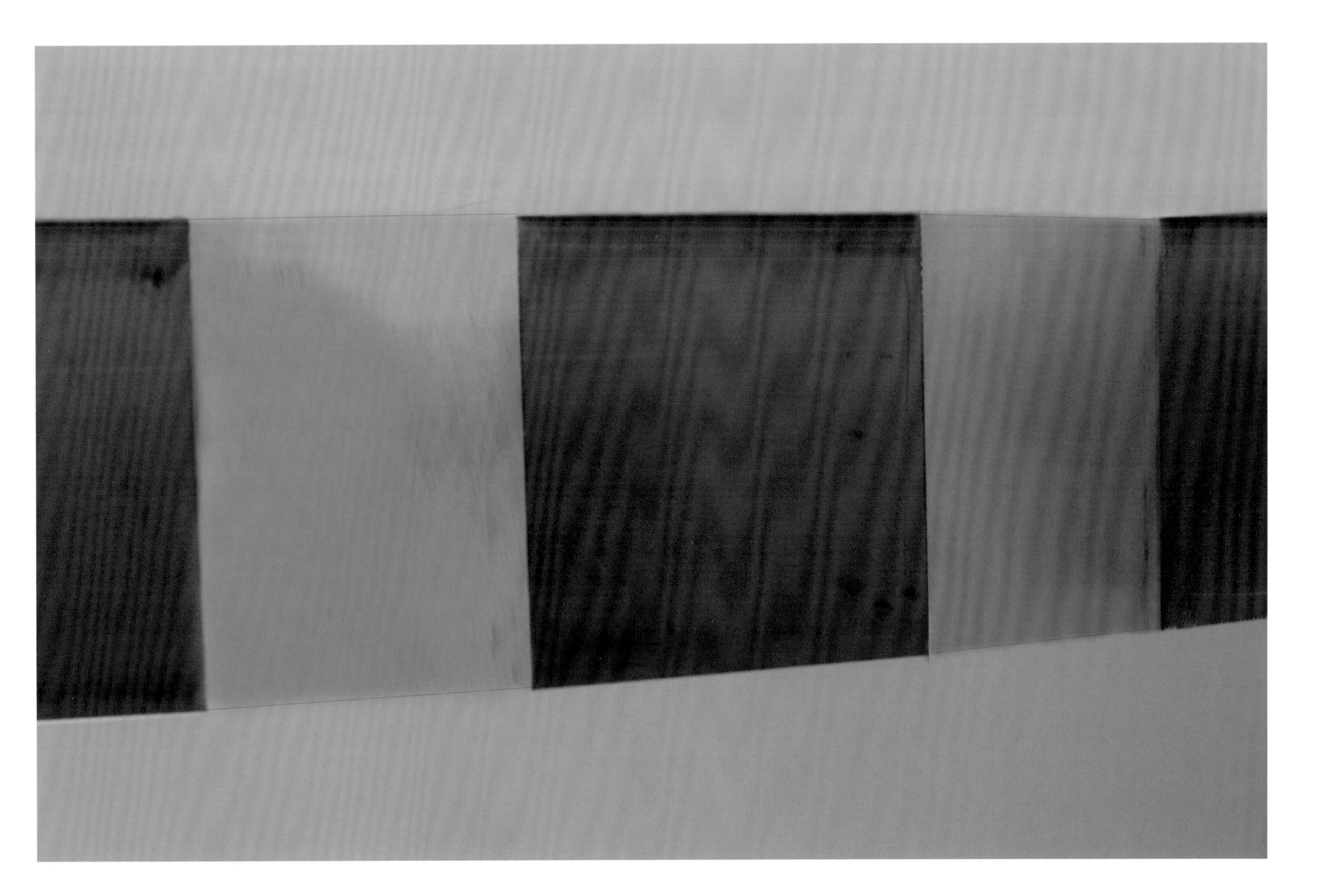

Sculpture XXIX (Wall V)
2019

Sculpture XXX
2019

Sculpture XXXI
2019

Sculpture XXXII
2019

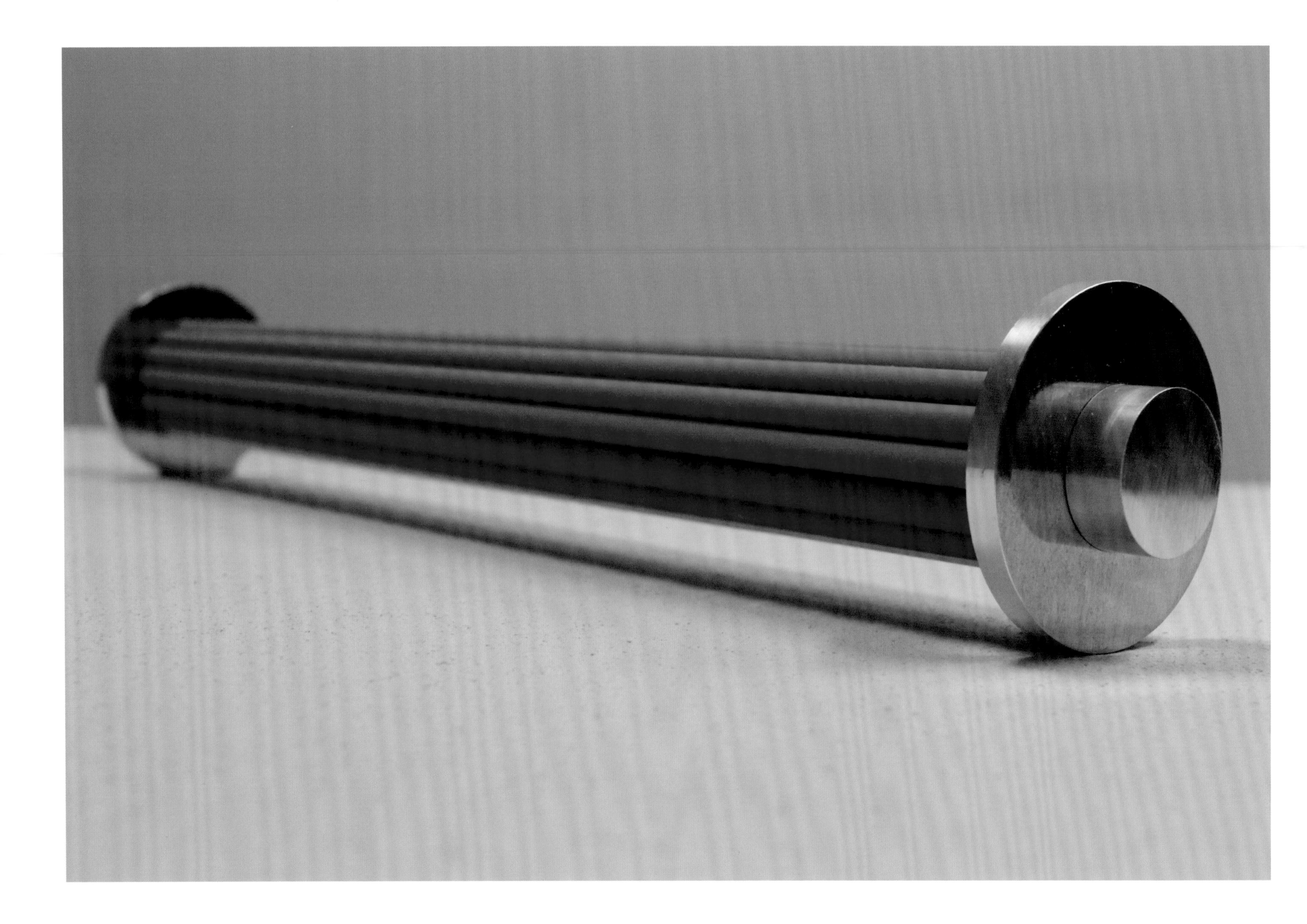

Sculpture XXXIII
2019

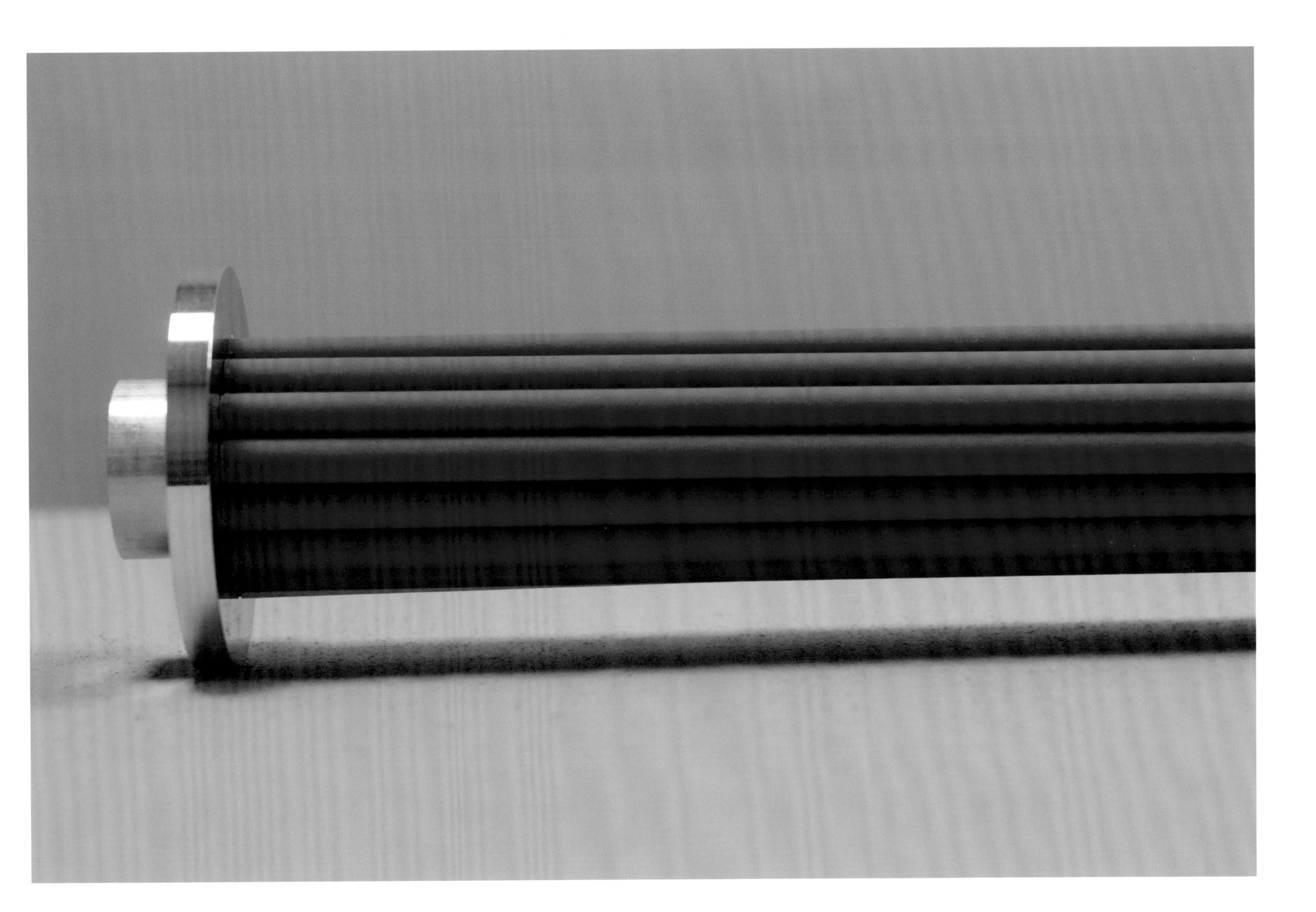

Sculpture XXXIII
2019

Sculpture XXXIII
2019

Sculpture XXXIV
2019

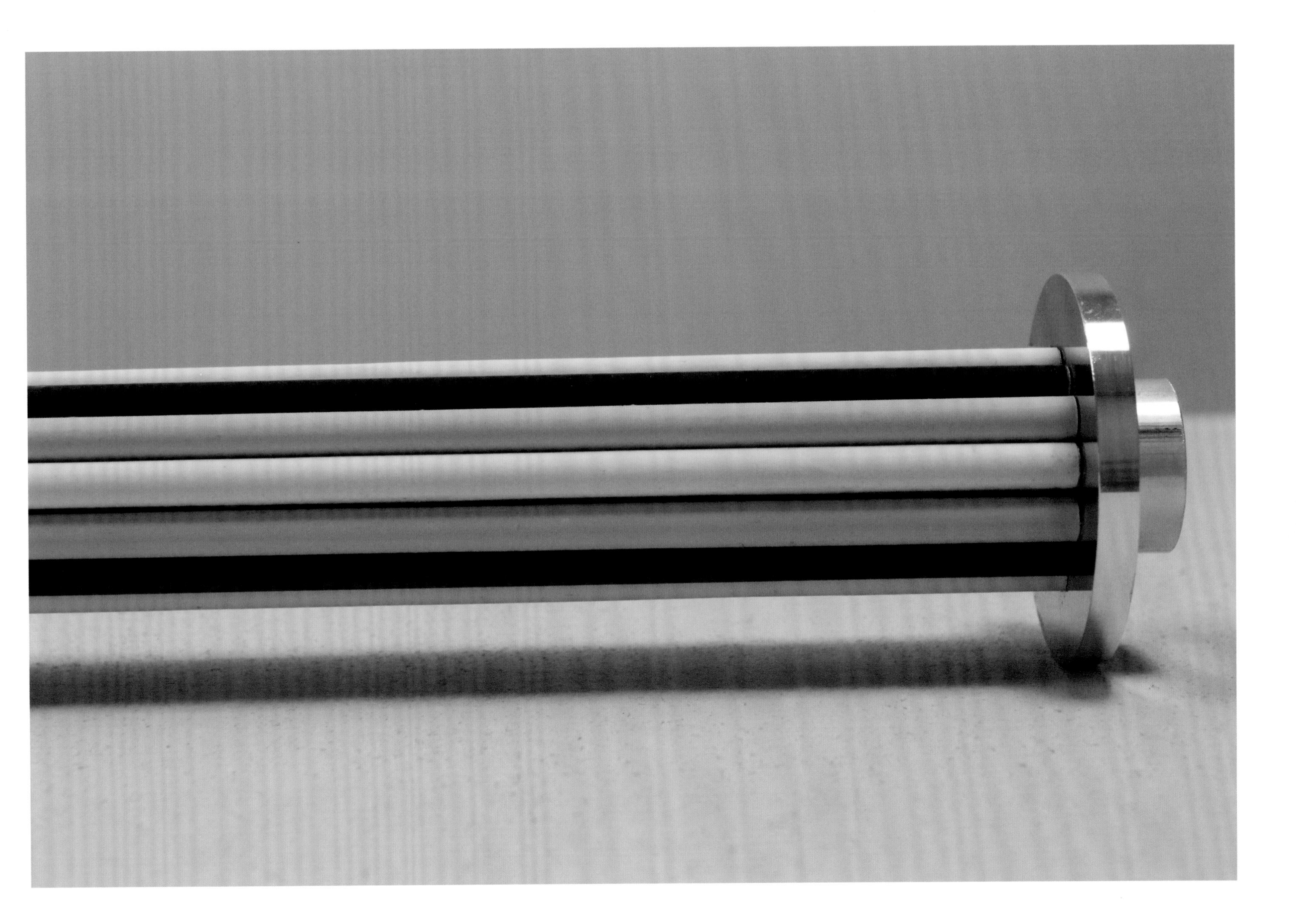

Sculpture XXXIV
2019

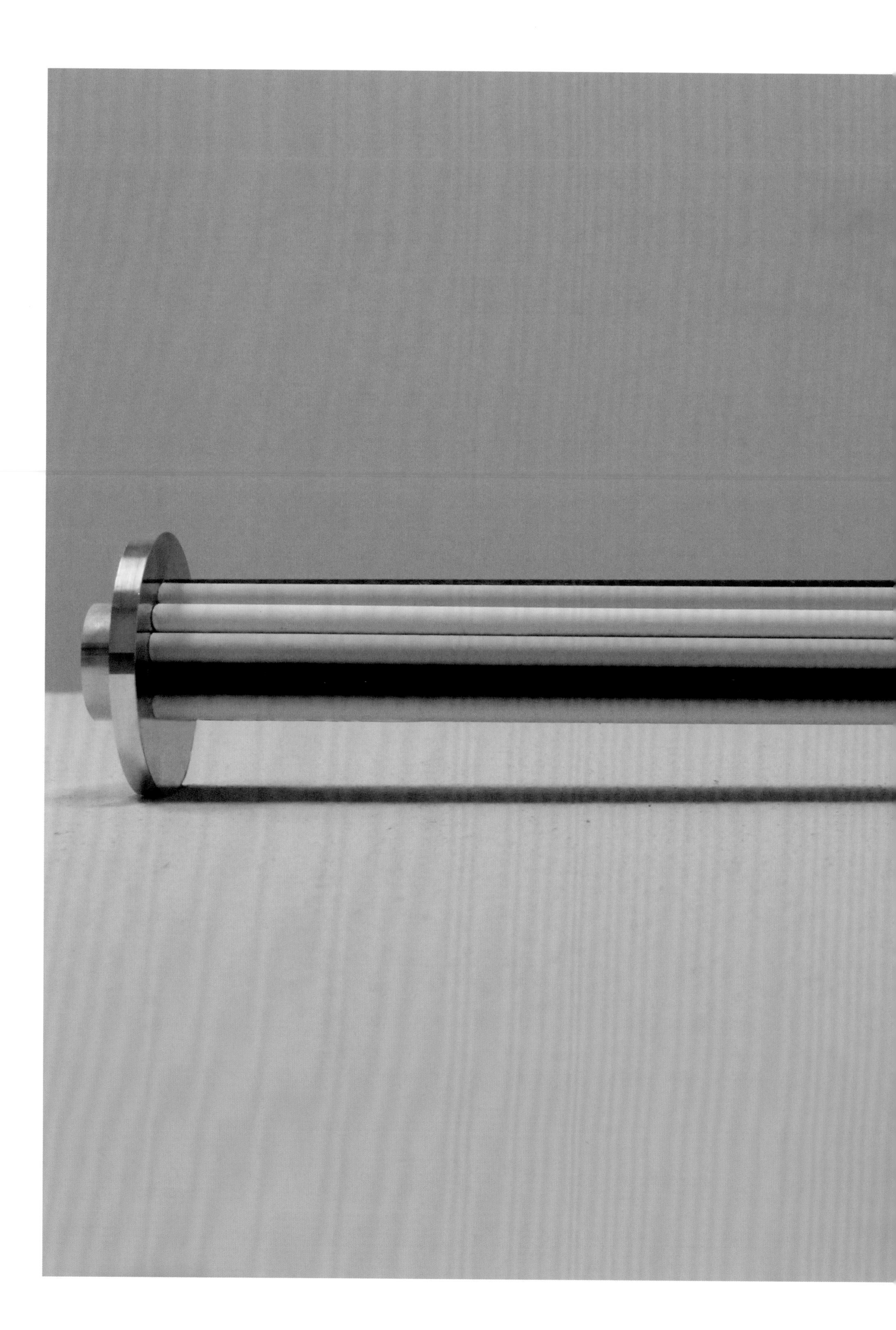

Sculpture XXXIV
2019

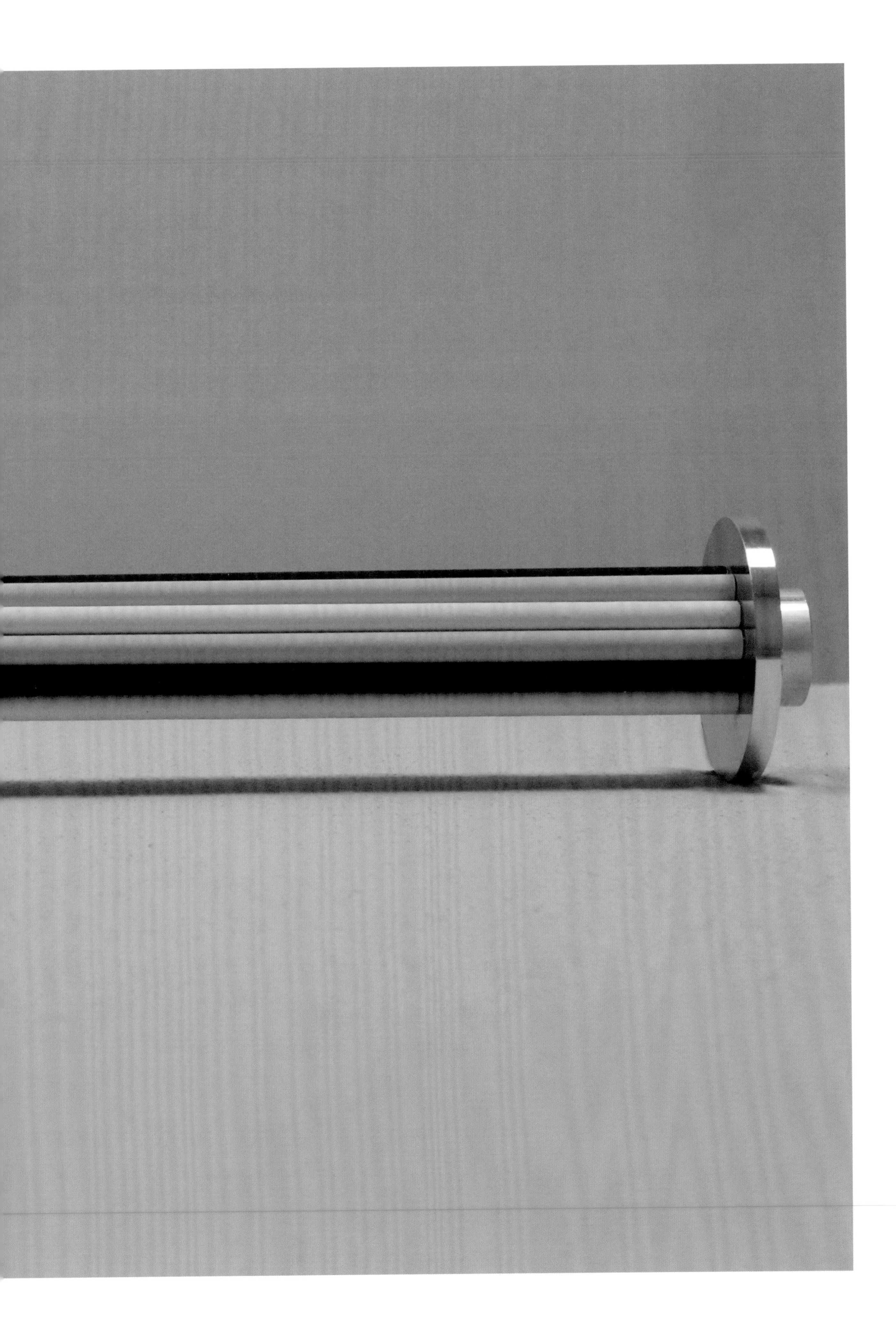

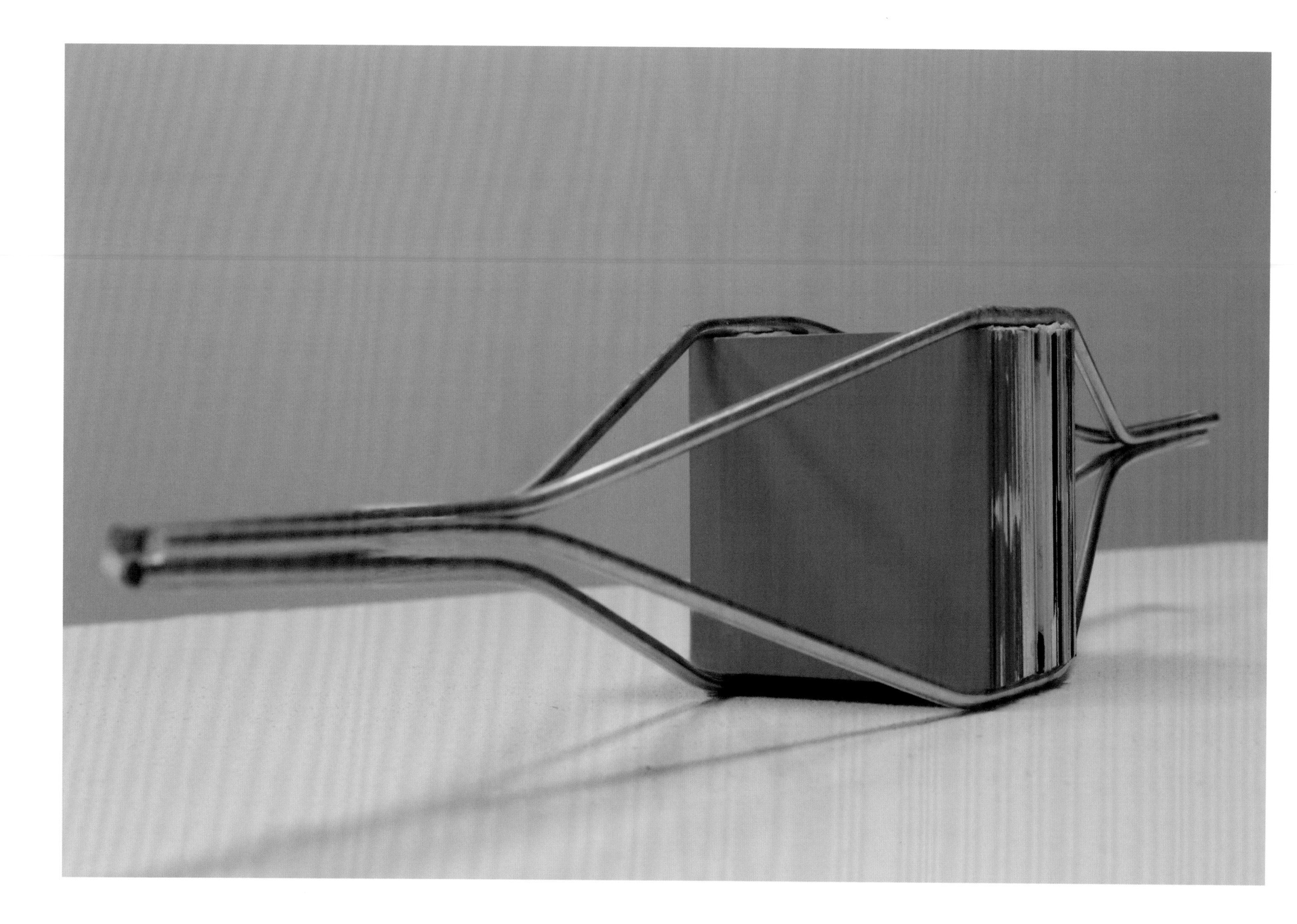

Sculpture XXXV
2019

Sculpture XXXV
2019

Sculpture XXXVI
2019

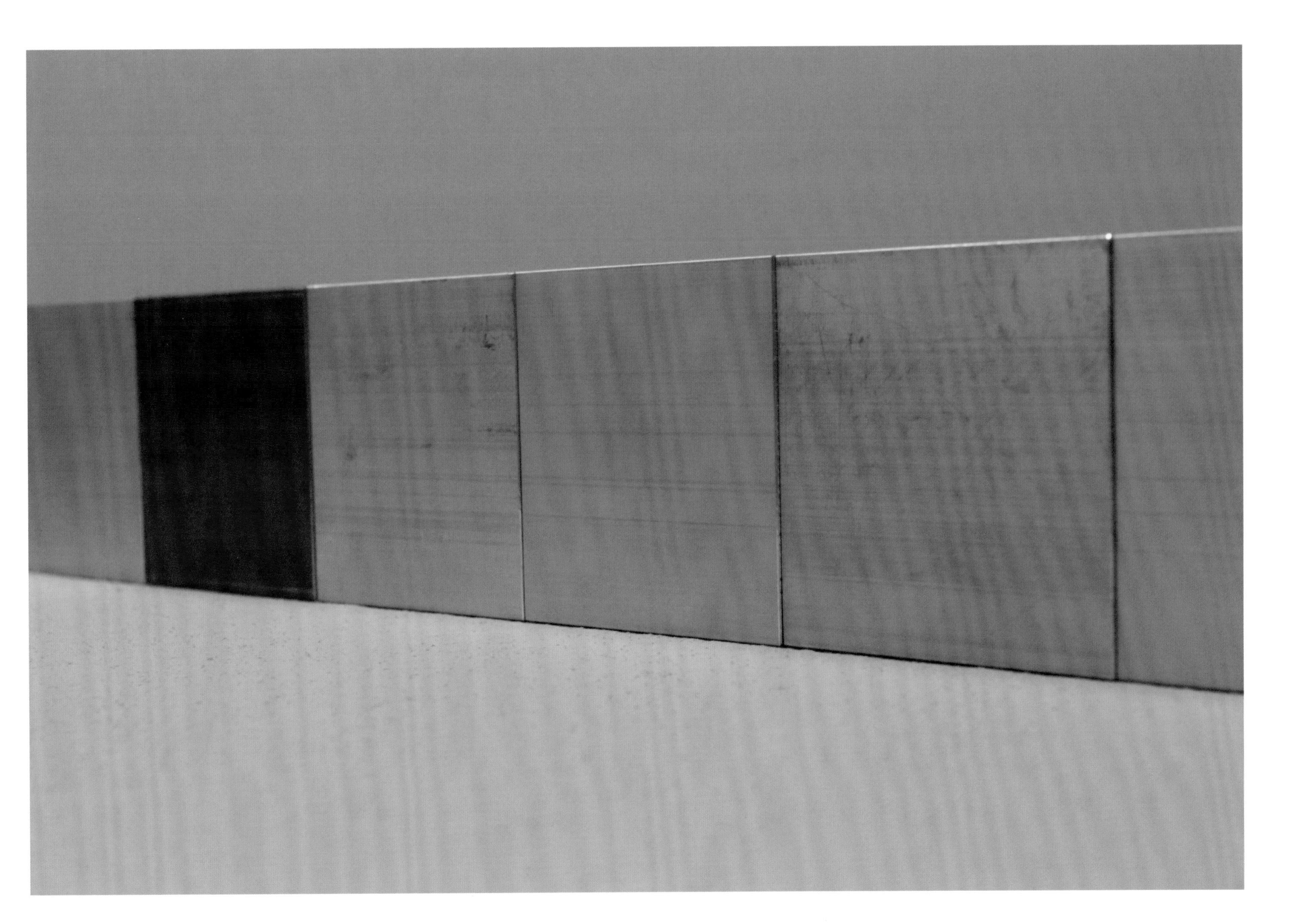

Sculpture XXXVI
2019

Sculpture XXXVII
2019

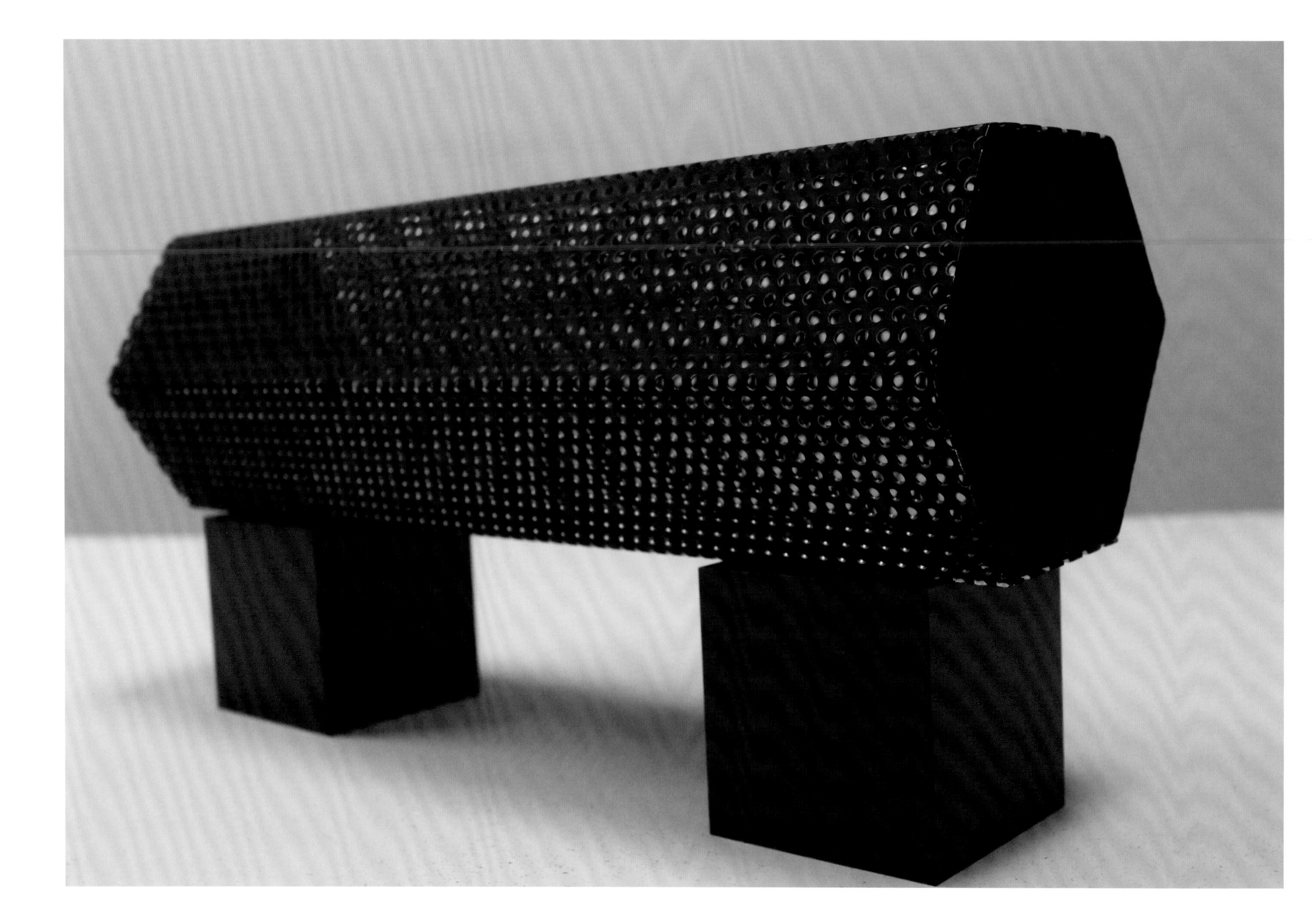

Sculpture XXXIX
2019

Sculpture XL
2019

Sculpture XL
2019

Sculpture XLI (Blue Cylinder)
2020

Sculpture XLII
2019

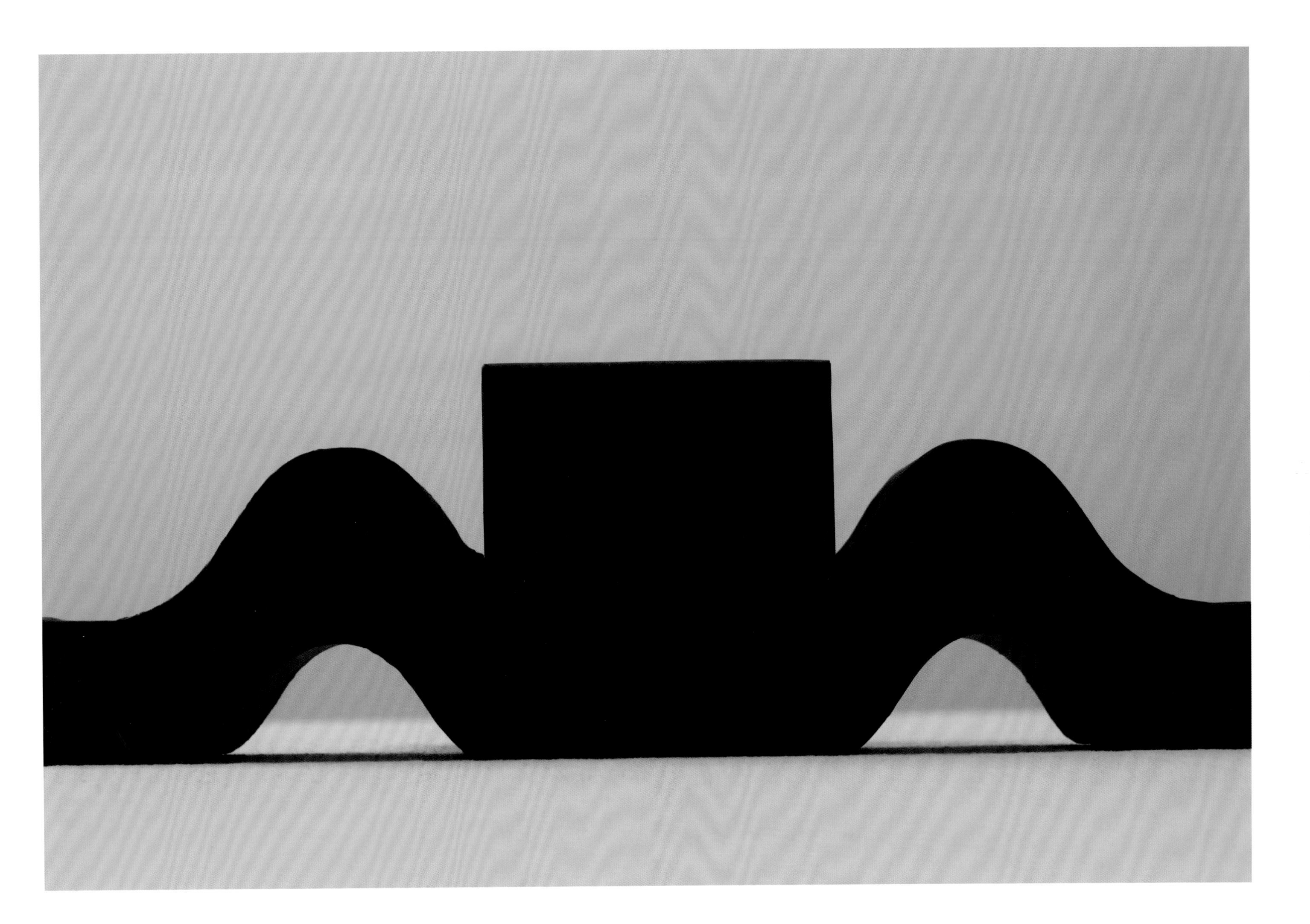

Sculpture XLII
2019

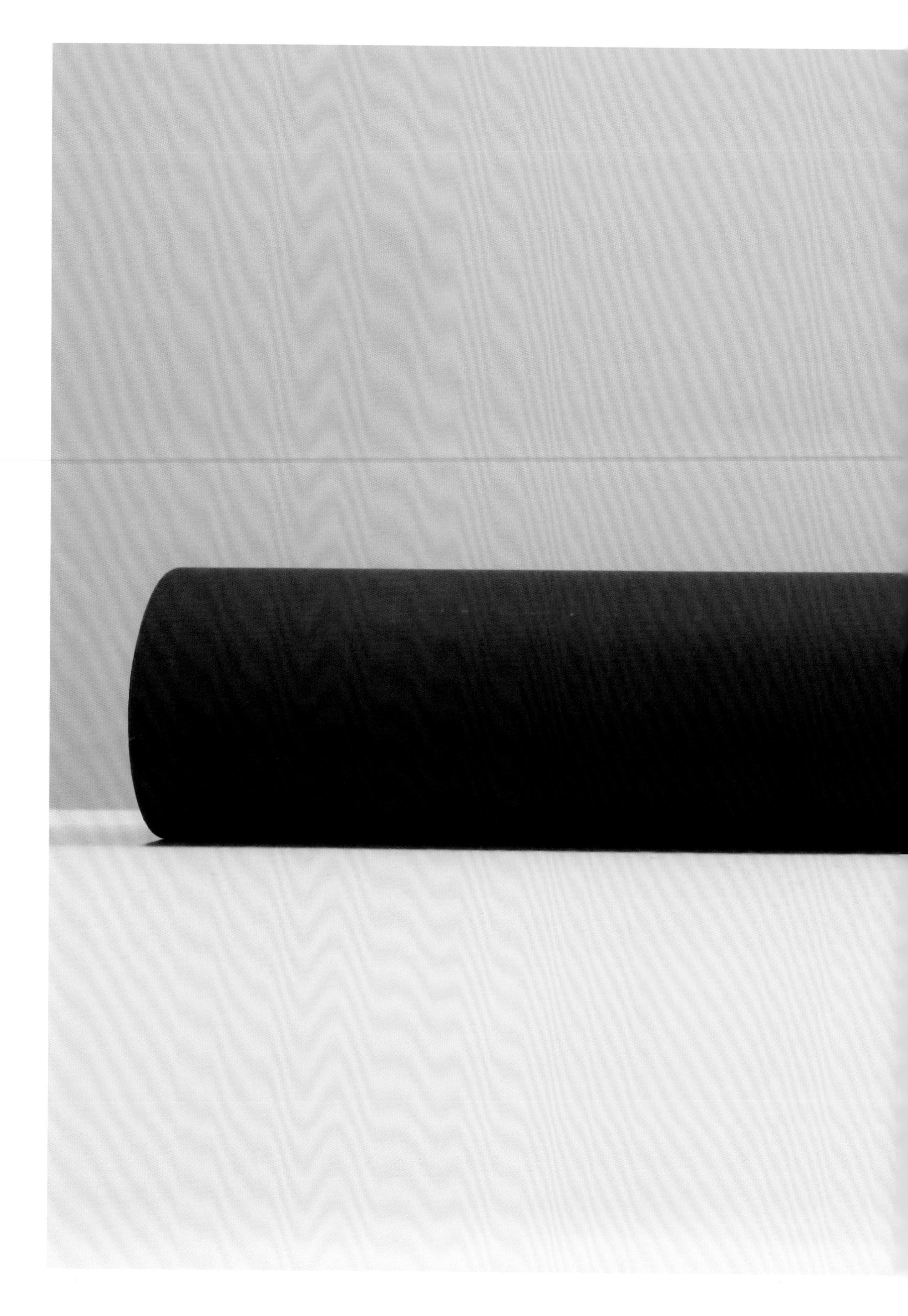

Sculpture XLIII
2019

Sculpture XLIII
2019

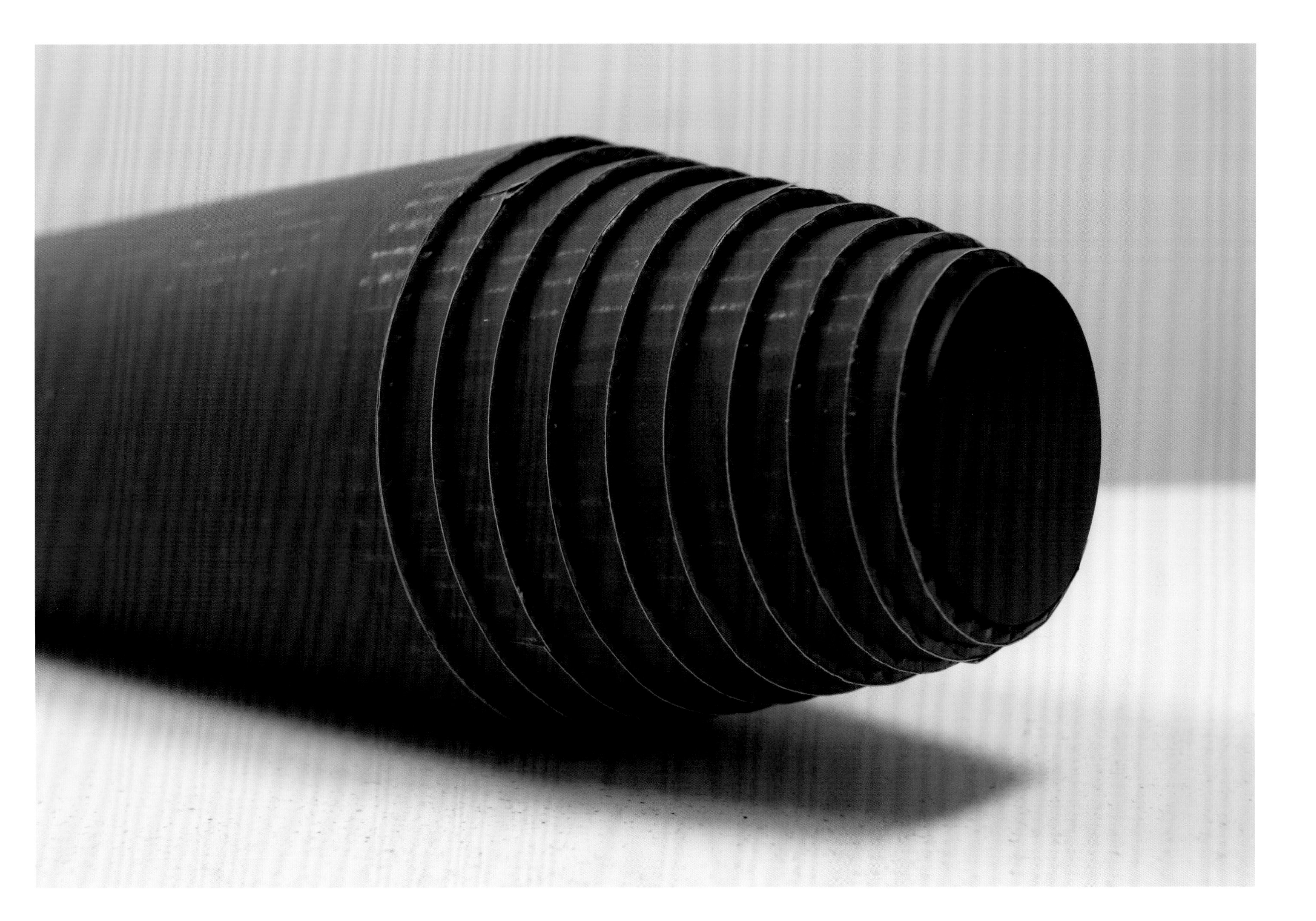

Sculpture XLIII
2019

Sculpture XLIV
2019

Sculpture XLIV
2019

Sculpture XLIV
2019

Sculpture XLV
2019

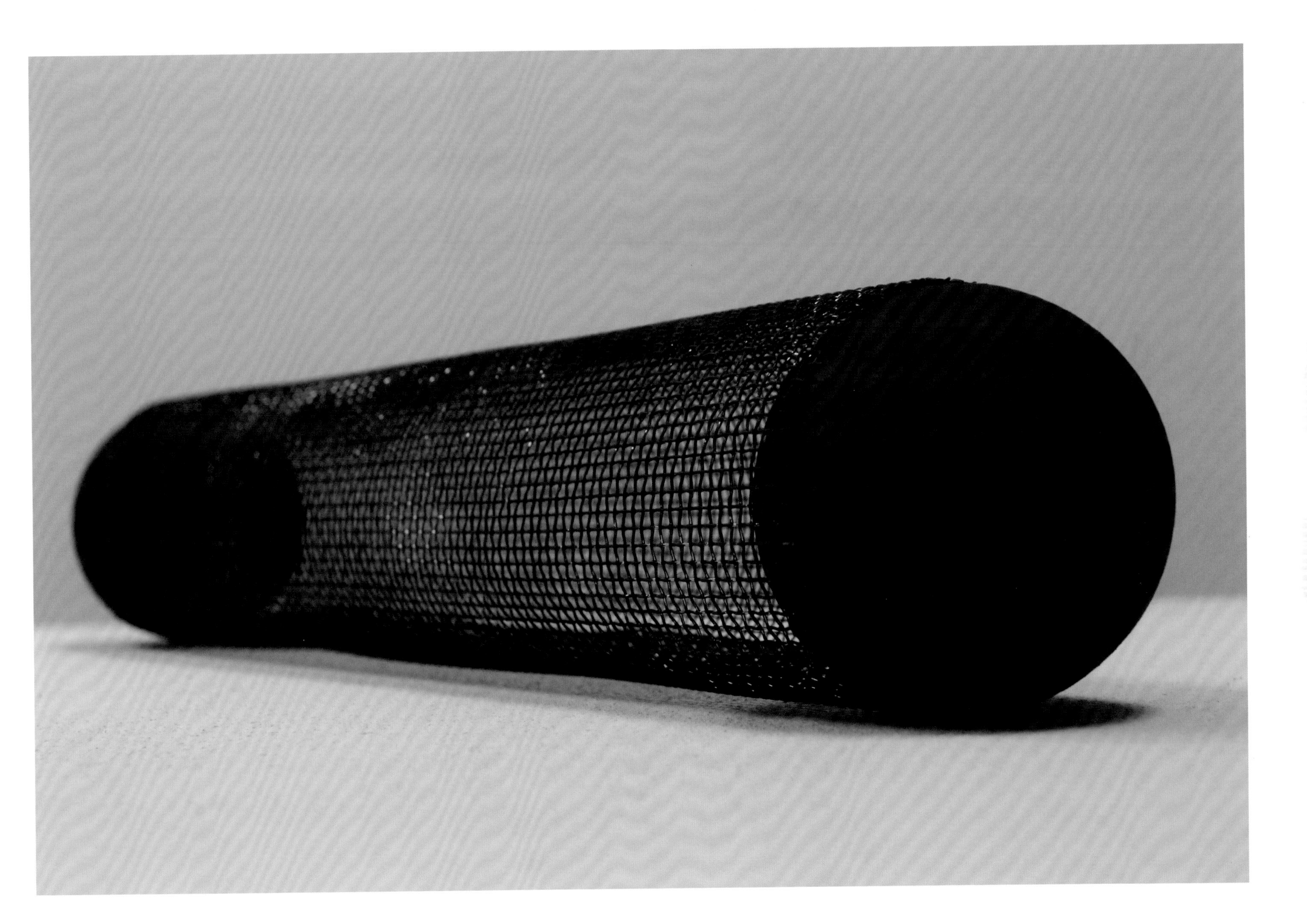

Sculpture XLVI
2019

Sculpture XLVI
2019

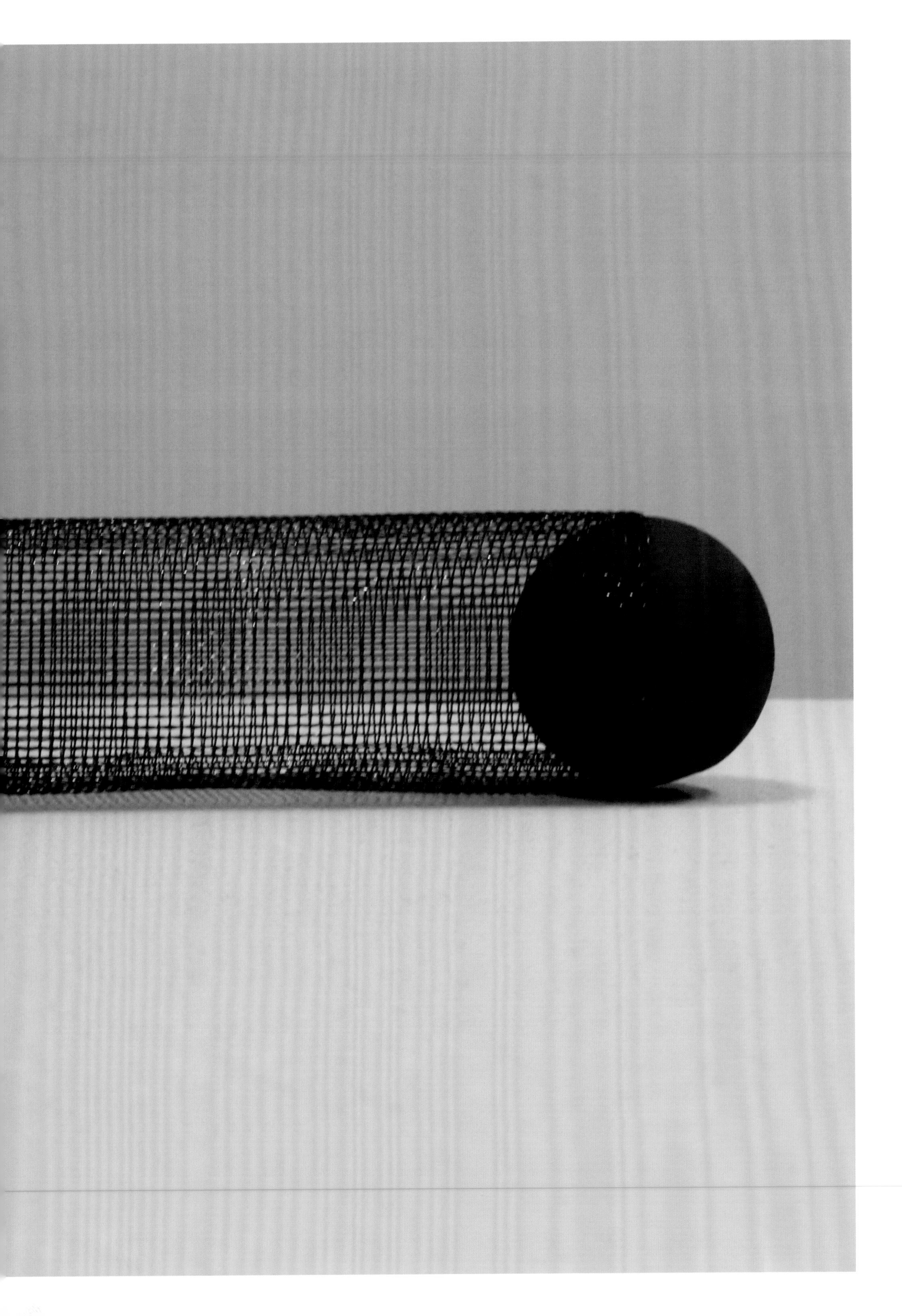

Sculpture XLVI
2019

Sculpture XLVII (The Big Bang Wheel)
2019

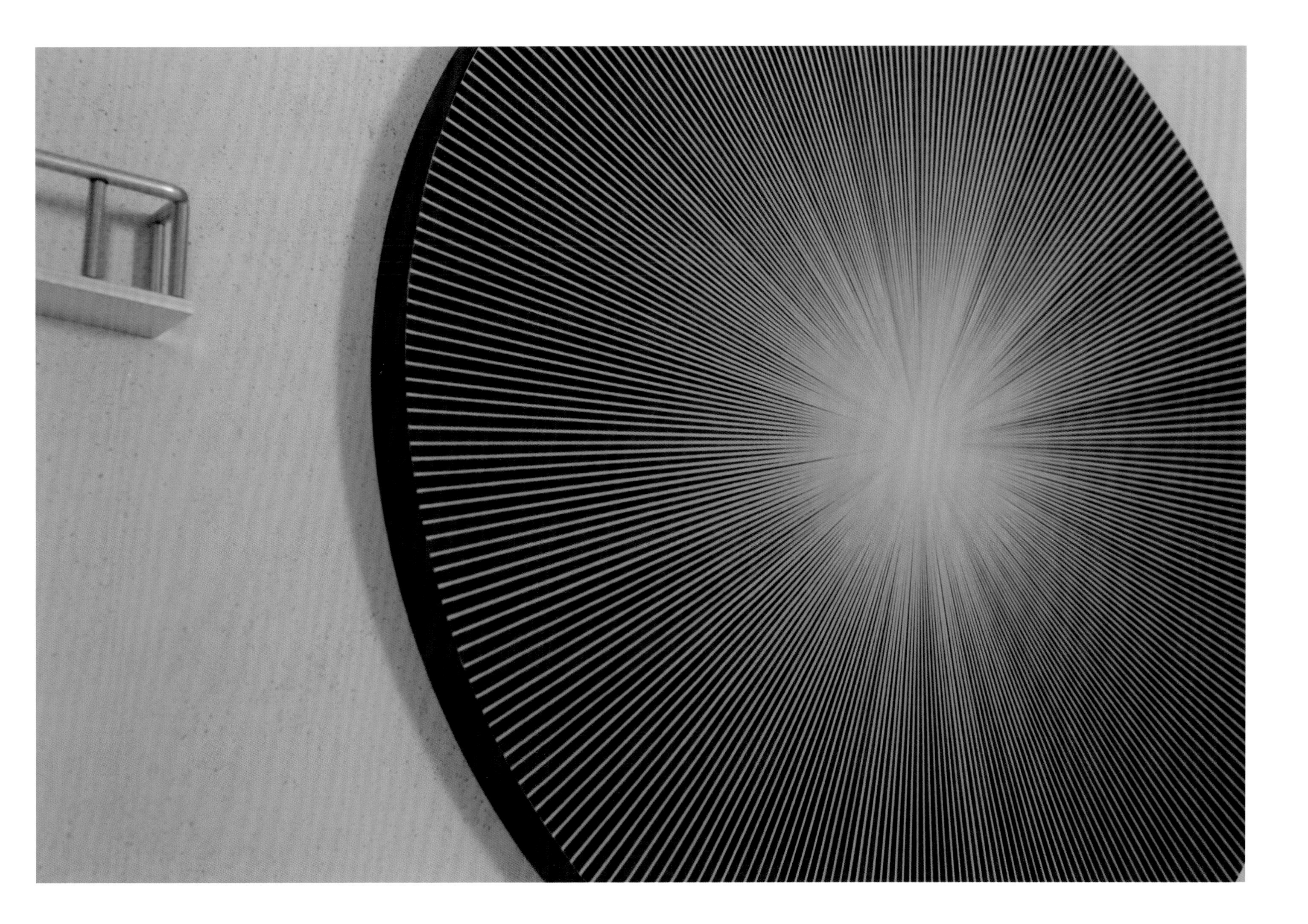

Sculpture XLVII (The Big Bang Wheel)
2019

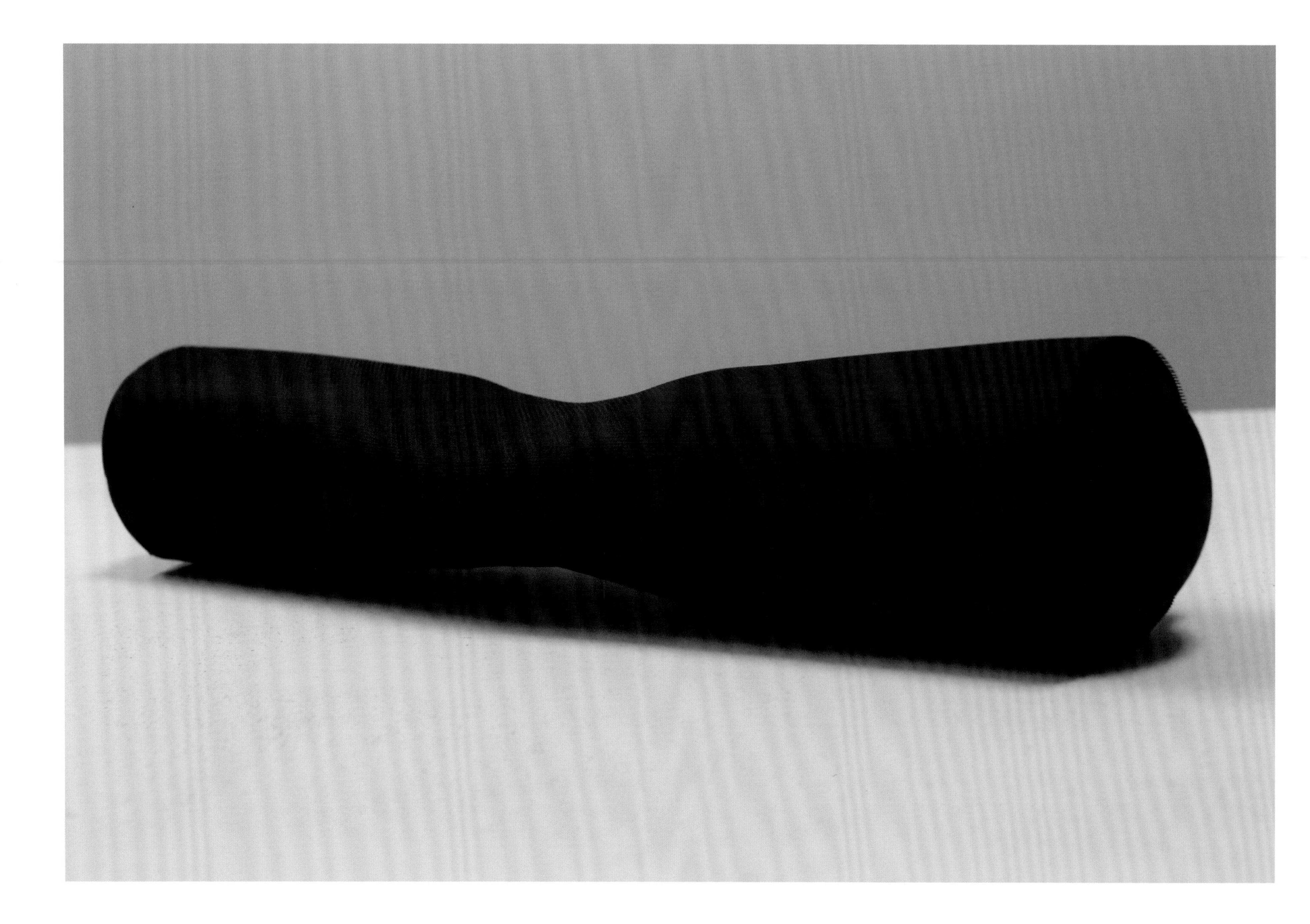

Sculpture XLVIII
2019

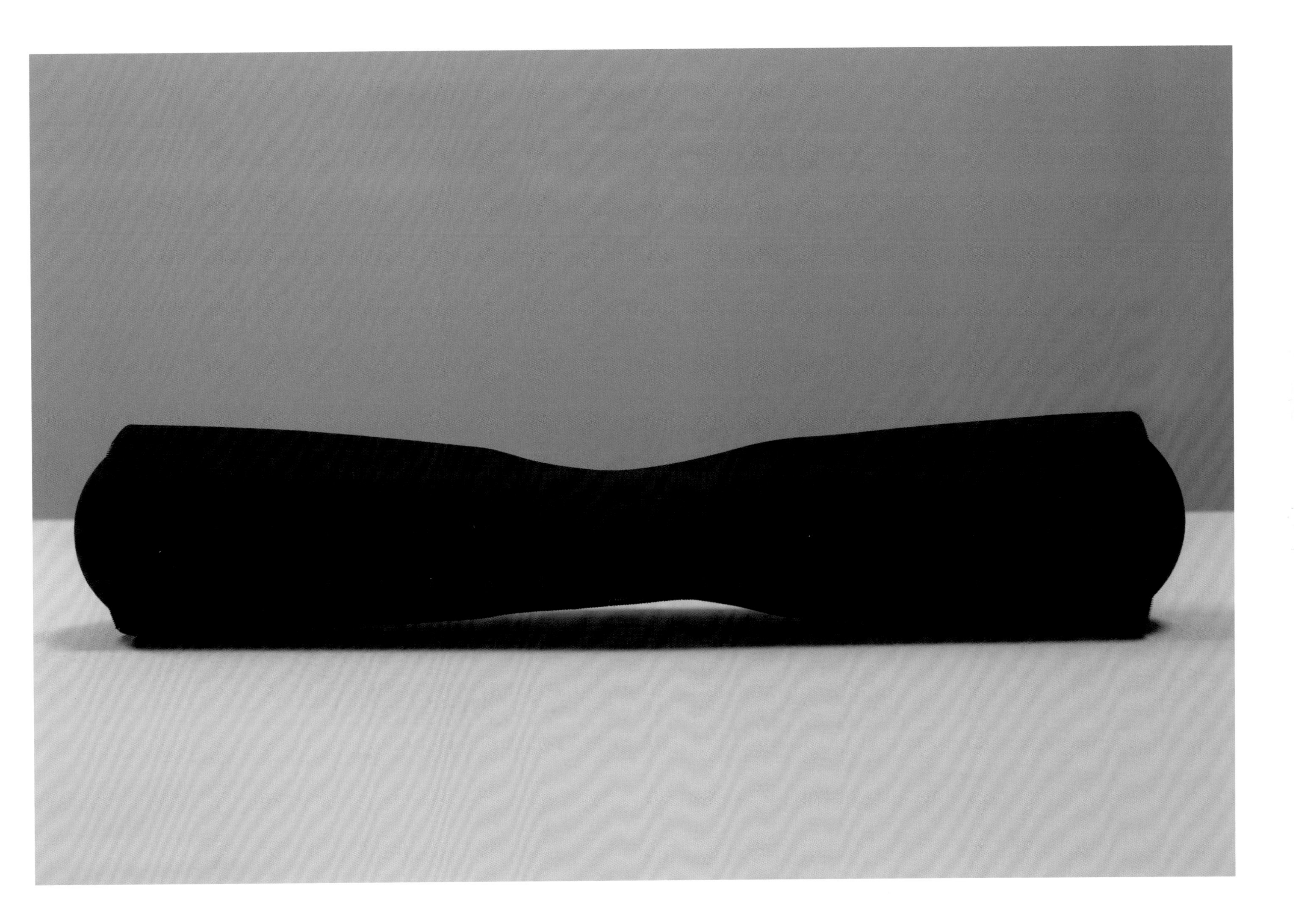

Sculpture XLVIII
2019

Sculpture XLIX
2019

Sculpture XLIX
2019

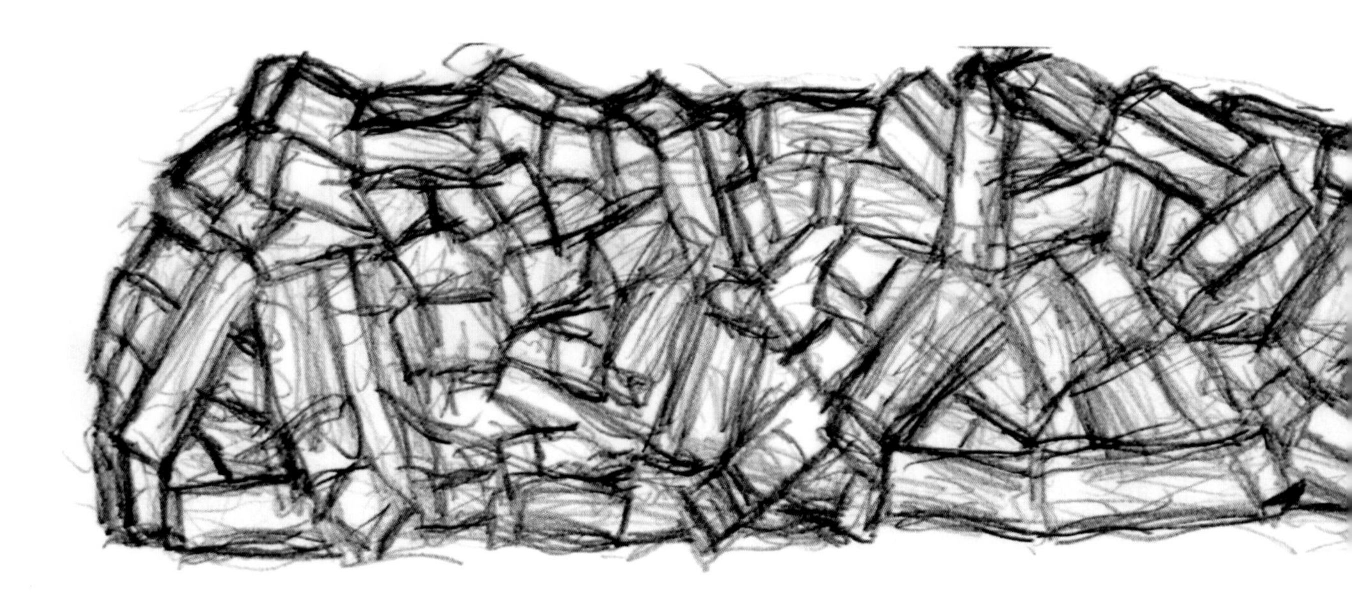

Sculpture L (Drawing)
2019

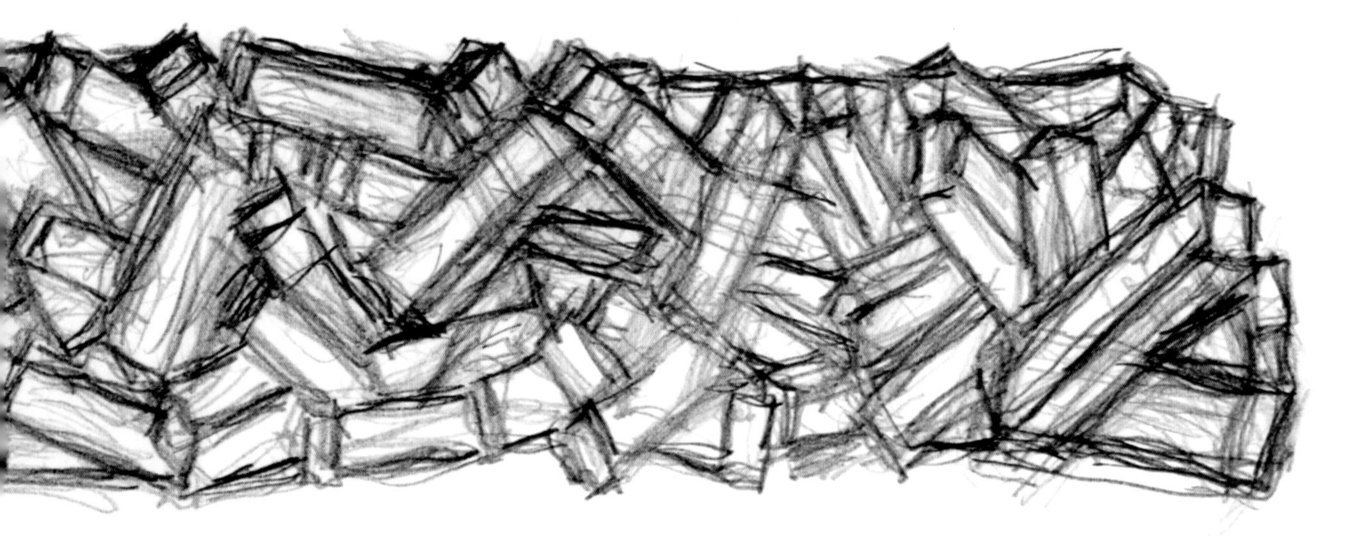

Sculpture LI
2019

Sculpture LI
2019

Sculpture LI
2019

Sculpture LI
2019

Sculpture LII
2019

Sculpture LII
2019

Sculpture LII
2019

Sculpture LII
2019

Sculpture LIII
2019

Sculpture LIV
(Big Cylinder)
2019

List of Works

Painting

p. 6
Black hole I
2019
acrylic on aluminum plate
diameter 90 cm / 35.4 in.

p. 7
Black hole XII
2019
acrylic on aluminum plate
diameter 90 cm / 35.4 in.

p. 8
The Big Bang I
2019
acrylic on aluminum plate
diameter 90 cm / 35.4 in.

p. 9
The Big Bang VII
2019
acrylic on aluminum plate
diameter 90 cm / 35.4 in.

p. 10
Black hole VI
2019
acrylic on aluminum plate
diameter 90 cm / 35.4 in.

p. 11
Black hole IX
2020
acrylic on aluminum plate
diameter 90 cm / 35.4 in.

p. 12
Black hole XI
2019
acrylic on aluminum plate
diameter 90 cm / 35.4 in.

p. 13
Black hole IV
2019
acrylic on aluminum plate
diameter 90 cm / 35.4 in.

p. 14
The Big Bang V
2019
acrylic on aluminum plate
diameter 90 cm / 35.4 in.

p. 15
Black hole III
2019
acrylic on aluminum plate
diameter 90 cm / 35.4 in.

p. 16
The Big Bang III
2019
acrylic on aluminum plate
diameter 90 cm / 35.4 in.

p. 17
The Big Bang II
2019
acrylic on aluminum plate
diameter 90 cm / 35.4 in.

p. 18
The Big Bang IV
2019
acrylic on aluminum plate
diameter 90 cm / 35.4 in.

p. 19
Black hole II
2019
acrylic on aluminum plate
diameter 90 cm / 35.4 in.

p. 20
The Big Bang VI
2019
acrylic on aluminum plate
diameter 90 cm / 35.4 in.

p. 21
The Big Bang IX
2019
acrylic on aluminum plate
diameter 90 cm / 35.4 in.

p. 22
Black hole V
2019
acrylic on aluminum plate
diameter 90 cm / 35.4 in.

p. 23
Small Black hole Yellow
2019
acrylic on aluminum plate
diameter 52 cm / 20.5 in.

p. 24-25
Five Black holes I, II, III, IV, V
2019
acrylic on aluminum plate
diameter 52 cm / 20.5 in., each

p. 26
Solar eclipse I
2019
acrylic on aluminum plate
diameter 90 cm / 35.4 in.

p. 27
Solar eclipse III
2019
acrylic on aluminum plate
diameter 90 cm / 35.4 in.

p. 28
Solar eclipse II
2019
acrylic on aluminum plate
diameter 90 cm / 35.4 in.

p. 31
Abstract Expressionism 21C VI
2019
acrylic on aluminum plate
83 x 71 cm / 32.7 x 28 in.

p. 32
Abstract Expressionism 21C IX
2019
acrylic on aluminum plate
83 x 71 cm / 32.7 x 28 in.

p. 33
Abstract Expressionism 21C VII
2019
acrylic on aluminum plate
83 x 71 cm / 32.7 x 28 in.

p. 34
Abstract Expressionism 21C VIII
2019
acrylic on aluminum plate
83 x 71 cm / 32.7 x 28 in.

p. 35
Abstract Expressionism 21C X
2019
acrylic on aluminum plate
83 x 71 cm / 32.7 x 28 in.

p. 36
Abstract Expressionism 21C XII
2019
acrylic on aluminum plate
60 x 40 cm / 23.6 x 15.7 in.

p. 37
Abstract Expressionism 21C XI
2019
acrylic on aluminum plate
60 x 40 cm / 23.6 x 15.7 in.

p. 38
Abstract Expressionism 21C XIII
2019
acrylic on aluminum plate
60 x 40 cm / 23.6 x 15.7 in.

p. 39
Abstract Expressionism 21C XIV
2019
acrylic on aluminum plate
60 x 40 cm / 23.6 x 15.7 in.

p. 40
Abstract Expressionism 21C I
2019
acrylic on aluminum plate
83 x 79 cm / 32.7 x 31.1 in.

p. 41
Abstract Expressionism 21C II
2019
acrylic on aluminum plate
83 x 79 cm / 32.7 x 31.1 in.

p. 42
Abstract Expressionism 21C IV
2019
acrylic on aluminum plate
83 x 79 cm / 32.7 x 31.1 in.

p. 43
Abstract Expressionism 21C V
2019
acrylic on aluminum plate
83 x 79 cm / 32.7 x 31.1 in.

p. 44
Abstract Expressionism 21C III
2019
acrylic on aluminum plate
83 x 79 cm / 32.7 x 31.1 in.

p. 47
Composition I
2019
acrylic on aluminum plate
36 x 36 cm / 14.2 x 14.2 in.

p. 48-49
Composition II, III, IV
2019
acrylic on aluminum plate
II: 9 x 54 cm / 3.5 x 21.3 in.
III: 12 x 72 cm / 4.7 x 28.3 in.
IV: 9 x 36 cm / 3.5 x 14.2 in.

p. 50
Frame Painting I
2019
acrylic on aluminum plate
26.2 x 38 cm / 10.3 x 15 in.

p. 51
Frame Painting II
2019
acrylic on aluminum plate
26.2 x 38 cm / 10.3 x 15 in.

p. 52
Frame Painting III
2019
acrylic on aluminum plate
26.2 x 38 cm / 10.3 x 15 in.

p. 53
Frame Painting IV
2019
acrylic on aluminum plate
26.2 x 38 cm / 10.3 x 15 in.

p. 55
Works on Paper Viridian Hue
2019
acrylic on cardboard
59.4 x 62.5 cm / 23.4 x 24.6 in.

p. 56-57
Black hole Drawing I, II, III
2019
acrylic on paper, inkjet print
diameter 25.7 cm / 10.1 in., each

Sculpture

p. 60-61
Sculpture XXVII (Wall III)
2019
aluminum, paint
12 x 84 x 0.5 cm / 4.7 x 33.1 x 0.2 in.

p. 62-63
Sculpture XXVIII (Wall IV)
2019
aluminum, paint
9 x 72 x 0.4 cm / 3.5 x 28.3 x 0.2 in.

p. 65
Sculpture XXIX (Wall V)
2019
aluminum, paint
12 x 60 x 0.5 cm / 4.7 x 23.6 x 0.2 in.

p. 66
Sculpture XXX
2019
aluminum, copper
5 x 5 x 5 cm / 2 x 2 x 2 in., each

p. 67
Sculpture XXXI
2019
aluminum, copper
5 x 28.5 x 7.7 cm / 2 x 11.2 x 3 in.

p. 69
Sculpture XXXII
2019
aluminum, cardboard, black gesso
9 x 26.5 x 9 cm / 3.5 x 10.4 x 3.5 in.

p. 70
Sculpture XXXIII
2019
aluminum, paint
4.8 x 32.3 x 4.8 cm / 1.9 x 12.7 x 1.9 in.

p. 71
Sculpture XXXIII

p. 72-73
Sculpture XXXIII

p. 74
Sculpture XXXIV
2019
aluminum, paint
4.8 x 32.3 x 4.8 cm / 1.9 x 12.7 x 1.9 in.

p. 75
Sculpture XXXIV

p. 76-77
Sculpture XXXIV

p. 78
Sculpture XXXV
2019
aluminum, paint
7.7 x 39.5 x 6.5 cm / 3 x 15.6 x 2.6 in.

p. 79
Sculpture XXXV

p. 80
Sculpture XXXVI
2019
aluminum, copper
5 x 35 x 5 cm / 2 x 13.8 x 2 in.

p. 81
Sculpture XXXVI

p. 82-83
Sculpture XXXVII
2019
anodized aluminum, aluminum, paint
31 x 32.5 x 31 cm / 12.2 x 12.8 x 12.2 in.

p. 84
Sculpture XXXIX
2019
aluminum bake-coated with acrylic resin, paint
14.8 x 30 x 10 cm / 5.8 x 11.8 x 3.9 in.

p. 85
Sculpture XL
2019
aluminum
5 x 38 x 4.4 cm / 2 x 15 x 1.7 in.

p. 86-87
Sculpture XL

p. 88-89
Sculpture XLI (Blue Cylinder)
2020
aluminum, paint
4 x 23.2 x 4 cm / 1.6 x 9.1 x 1.6 in.

p. 90
Sculpture XLII
2019
aluminum, cardboard, black gesso
7.5 x 25.3 x 7 cm / 3 x 10 x 2.8 in.

p. 91
Sculpture XLII

p. 92-93
Sculpture XLIII
2019
anodized aluminum, cardboard, paint
8.6 x 50.5 x 8.6 cm / 3.4 x 19.9 x 3.4 in.

p. 94
Sculpture XLIII

p. 95
Sculpture XLIII

p. 96
Sculpture XLIV
2019
anodized aluminum, aluminum
11.4 x 38 x 31 cm / 4.5 x 15 x 12.2 in.

p. 97
Sculpture XLIV

p. 98-99
Sculpture XLIV

p. 100
Sculpture XLV
2019
polystyrene ball, black gesso
diameter 6 cm / 2.4 in., each

p. 101
Sculpture XLVI
2019
aluminum mesh, polystyrene ball, paint, black gesso
6.2 x 35 x 6.2 cm / 2.4 x 13.8 x 2.4 in.

p. 102-103
Sculpture XLVI

p. 105
Sculpture XLVI

p. 106-107
Sculpture XLVII (The Big Bang Wheel)
2019
acrylic on aluminum
31 x 31 x 1.5 cm / 12.2 x 12.2 x 0.6 in.

p. 109
Sculpture XLVII (The Big Bang Wheel)

p. 110
Sculpture XLVIII
2019
aluminum mesh, polystyrene ball, black gesso
6 x 32.5 x 7.7 cm / 2.4 x 12.8 x 3 in.

p. 111
Sculpture XLVIII

p. 112-113
Sculpture XLIX
2019
aluminum
5 x 32.3 x 5 cm / 2 x 12.7 x 2 in.

p. 114-115
Sculpture XLIX

p. 116-117
Sculpture L (Drawing)
2019
pencil on paper
21 x 29.7 cm / 8.3 x 11.7 in.

p. 118-119
Sculpture LI
2019
wood, black gesso
6 x 47 x 12 cm / 2.4 x 18.5 x 4.7 in.

p. 120
Sculpture LI

p. 121
Sculpture LI

p. 122
Sculpture LI

p. 124-125
Sculpture LII
2019
wood, black gesso
3.7 x 36.3 x 5.1 cm / 1.5 x 14.3 x 2 in.

p. 126
Sculpture LII

p. 127
Sculpture LII

p. 128
Sculpture LII

p. 131
Sculpture LIII
2019
aluminum, wood, black gesso
23.2 x 45 x 14 cm / 9.1 x 17.7 x 5.5 in.

p. 132-133
Sculpture LIV（Big Cylinder）
2019
aluminum, paint
4 x 18.5 x 4 cm / 1.6 x 7.3 x 1.6 in.

Brief history of the artist

Eizo Nishio: b.1953, Tokyo. / Graduated from the Faculty of Economics, Sophia University, Tokyo, and studied Social Sciences at Waseda University, Tokyo. / Exhibited at Textile as Sculpture, 12th International Biennial of Tapestry at Cantonal Museum of Fine Arts, Lausanne, Switzerland, 1985, and KUNSTEN - Museum of Modern Art Aalborg, Denmark, 1985. / Established Art & Books in Tokyo, 1987. / Writes articles and comments for all periodicals published by Art & Books. / Published ***20/21C ART BOOKS***, 2010, ***Eizo Nishio: Sculptures & Drawings 2011-2014***, 2014, ***Eizo Nishio: Paintings. Square and Long Rectangle***, 2015, and other books.

Eizo Nishio
Paintings 2014
Art & Books

Editing by Eizo Nishio
Photographs by Eizo Nishio

ISBN 978-4-909594-12-9

Art & Books Publishers, Tokyo
www.artbibliography.com